EDITOR: **DAVID PORTER**

Compiled from the 1995 London Lectures on Contemporary Christianity organised by
Julia Bicknell, Senior Broadcast Journalist, BBC News and Current Affairs

Copyright © 1997 The Institute for Contemporary Christianity

First Published 1997 by Paternoster Press

03 02 01 00 99 98 97   7 6 5 4 3 2 1

Paternoster Press is an imprint of Paternoster Publishing,
P.O. Box 300, Carlisle, Cumbria CA3 0QS

The right of the contributors to be identified as the Authors of this Work has been asserted by them in accordance with the Copyright, Designs and Patents Act 1988.

All rights reserved. No part of this publication may be reproduced, stored in a retrieval system, or transmitted in any form or by any means, electronic, mechanical, photocopying, recording or otherwise, without the prior permission of the publisher or a licence permitting restricted copying. In the U.K. such licences are issued by the Copyright Licensing Agency, 90 Tottenham Court Road, London W1P 9HE.

British Library Cataloguing in Publication Data

A catalogue record for this book is available from the British Library.

ISBN 0-85364-794-1

This book is printed using Suffolk New Book paper which is 100% acid free.

Typeset by WestKey Limited, Falmouth, Cornwall
Printed in Great Britain by Clays Ltd., Bungay, Suffolk

CONTENTS

Editor's Preface	vii
1. Public Broadcasting — Servant or Leader? *Robert McLeish, Director, Robert McLeish Associates Management and Media Training Consultancy*	1
2. Is More News Good News? *Justin Phillips, Daily News Programmes, BBC Radio*	23
3. Never Mind the Quality, Feel the Ratings! *Graham Mytton, Head of Audience Research and Correspondence, BBC*	53
4. The Age of Information — The Electronic Classroom? *Alan Rogers, Independent Consultant, and Programme Director of ARK2*	74
5. Religious Broadcasting — For the Nation or the Ghetto? *Tim Dean, Commissioning Editor, Independent Productions, BBC World Service*	87
Index	105

Editor's Preface

The five chapters of this symposium contain the text of the five 1995 London Lectures. At a time of major change in British broadcasting, these contributions by Christians at a senior level in broadcasting provided an informative and also a prophetic insight, as each in turn not only identified the processes of change but discussed the underlying factors and issues that were driving the changes.

For this reason, the lectures remain as relevant as when they were delivered. However, all the lecturers have taken the opportunity of revising matters of detail and updating their text as appropriate. Although these changes obviously enhance the text, it has not been the intention of the authors or the publishers to make the present volume as comprehensively up-to-date as were the original lectures. The book remains essentially a transcript of the lectures as given and now edited for publication; quite apart from the fact that its value lies primarily in general analysis rather than in specific data, a comprehensively revised text could only reflect the situation as of late 1996 and would itself soon be out of date in its turn.

The contributors have in some cases moved on to other positions in the media since May 1995; the credits against their contributions in the present book are taken from the original lecture programme.

The London Lectures, which have been delivered annually since 1974, are organised by the London Lectures Committee under the auspices of the Institute for Contemporary Christianity, St Peter's Church, Vere Street, London W1M 9HP, from whom tapes of recent lectures can be obtained.

David Porter

1: Public Broadcasting — Servant or Leader?

Robert McLeish

INTRODUCTION

Eighteen and a half years ago I sat in the audience for the London Lectures, then held at All Souls Langham Place, and listened to Malcolm Muggeridge talk about 'Christ and the Media'. Witty, erudite, well-storied with eminent people, he was both entertaining — and extremely critical. He had hardly a good word to say for the media, television in particular. His lectures struck me then (as they do now, for I have been re-reading them) as a savage and I have to say largely unwarranted attack on the hand, not to say the body, which had fed him and which to an extent gave him his public eminence in the 1960s and 70s. He was doing exactly what he was criticising the media for doing — being partial, exaggerating to the point of fantasy and overruling others' views for the sake of effect. That is why his lectures were so *interesting*. They had impact. We can still remember his parodied reportage of Christ as 'the honourable member for Galilee South', and his 'Dead Sea video tapes'. Yes, they are worth reading again; especially for style, but for content too. We are still asking the same questions about who sets the agenda and the moral standards for public communication.

In his analysis and in his views Muggeridge was so provocative, and so infuriating, because he was so unbalanced. Well, you won't get that from me, for my approach is — I won't say 'more considered', but it is balanced. And the trouble with balance is that it tends either to be inconclusive or frankly boring. But let me describe to you two different kinds of balance. The first is when you weigh everything up and decide to adopt a centralist position, and you stay there as if at the middle of a see-saw. The second (and this is where I am) is where balance means exploring the various extremities equally; first one end of the see-saw and then the other. For me it represents a love-hate relationship with broadcasting which has given me as a modest practitioner, trainer, and manager over thirty years enormous pleasures as well as problems. And as a consumer listener/viewer, it has given me exactly the same.

At one moment the media are the essential life-blood of a well-informed and cultured society; at the next they seem trivial and utterly disposable. People see in the media what they want to see, even from the identical data. It's like the story of a man on the seashore who found a stray dog and threw a stick for it into the sea. And off the dog went, down to the water. But instead of going into the sea, it trotted across the top of it, picked up the stick, ran back across the water, and dropped the stick at the man's feet. The man, amazed, did it again with the same result. Hardly able to believe his eyes, he called another man to come and see. He threw the stick for the dog again, and exactly the same thing happened; the dog walked over the water and brought the stick back. 'That's astounding,' said the second man. 'Absolutely astonishing! That's the first time I've ever seen a dog who couldn't swim.'

Our interpretation of what we see is very personal. It's mediated through all of life's other experiences. When I was working with the Commonwealth Broadcasting Secretariat as it then was[1], we all visited a teashop in Windsor. I remember thinking of the awesome power of broadcasting, certainly in terms of quantity; for here, in these very ordinary surroundings, were programme directors who were actually speaking to a quarter of the globe. On another occasion Frank Gillard gave me a timely reminder of the overriding importance of the relationship with the audience. It was 1968 at Radio Nottingham. We'd just had a stunt as part of the University Rag Week in which we pretended that the station had been taken over by students — in fact it brought the police round in force to protect us. The Press Association had got wind of it and the situation was beginning to get out of control. Frank took a typically benign view of it, but he did say:, 'Always be very careful how you spoof your audience. It's a relationship that you need'.

Later as Chairman of the BBC's Senior Management Conference for six years I must have heard every single broadcasting argument

---

[1] Now the Commonwealth Broadcasting Association.

in the context of its time — from Deputy Director General Alan Protheroe saying, 'Mark my words, in a few years it won't be *if* footballers have sponsors' names on their shirts, the argument will be over the size of the letters', to my question to Director General Alasdair Milne: 'Don't you think the BBC is sometimes rather arrogant?' and his classic response — 'It's very difficult not to be when you are the best'!

Now my task in the first of these 1995 lectures is to take something of an overview: to look at broadcasting in its role as a public servant, and to ask whether it can, or should, also lead public opinion; and if so, by what right and in which direction that leadership is to be. I also want to look at some current trends and implications, and attempt a Christian response to take us into the future. I shall also sound six warnings.

THE SERVANT ROLE

So, let us first of all look at the servant role. To simplify matters, it is helpful, I think, to analyse the function of the domestic servant, the butler or maid. And lest this seem quaintly old fashioned, we have to remind ourselves that everywhere we look in the 1990s the idea of service provision is thoroughly up to date. The Patient's Charter in the NHS, Passenger Charters in British Rail — indeed my own local council produces documents that more than ever clarify what it means by being a service provider. As manufacturing industry declines, so more and more jobs move into the service sector: from financial services, banking and catering, to education and training, entertainment and leisure. The ideas of customer service are now very much in vogue, although I have to say that when I set up the BBC's first Management Training Department in 1983 I called it the Management Training Service, because I saw its role as essentially providing a development and skills service for managers. It was some time before I realised how much the staff in the Department disliked the idea of being a service. It had connotations of being servile; it was demeaning. The name has changed now; but perhaps there is a perceived difference between providing a service and being a servant. But as I will argue, the one who genuinely serves, also leads. I think the Americans are better at this than we are. You can get terrific service in a restaurant together with the feeling that it is a great pleasure for the waitress or waiter to serve you — in fact they are often called 'servers'.

Let us look at the specific functions or attributes of the domestic servant, and then I will link their relevance to broadcasting as a service. I have identified ten, although there may be more. I listed them first in 1988 in my book, *Radio Production*, and expanded them further in the recent third edition[2].

First, *the perfect servant is unswervingly loyal* — loyal to the employer or family for whom they are working. The servant does not use this position of trust or privilege for his or her own ends, but is single-minded in service and does not attempt also to serve other interests. Servants are clear about their purpose and demonstrate this in everything they do.

Second, *our servant thoroughly understands the nuances and foibles of the family which he or she serves* — the culture, if you like, of the immediate environment. He is not critical or judgemental but understands individual weaknesses of character and behaviour. Broadly he accepts them, but if necessary he asks questions about them, perhaps challenges them, and *in extremis* may attempt to restrain them. But he is not a policeman, he has no prescriptive mandate. And neither is our servant a doormat to do whatever he is bidden, with no opinions of his own. This was, you may remember, one of the subtleties of Ishiguro's book *Remains of the Day*[3]. He asks to what extent a servant should turn a blind eye to what is going on. This is indeed a delicate line to tread.

Third, *a servant of excellence is available when needed and for whoever in the family requires help* — the young and the old as well as the head of the house. It may be tempting to pay court to the most influential of the household, to keep in with the paymaster, the powerful — but actually it may be that it is the children, the sick, or the disadvantaged who require most attention.

Fourth, our servant actually serves. He performs useful tasks, meeting stated needs and furthermore, anticipating requirements and problems so being ready to offer original and new solutions to situations as, or even before, they arise. The servant is not being merely reactive therefore, although this is critically important, but is looking ahead. He is *useful and creative*.

---

[2] Robert McLeish, *Radio Production* (Focal Press, 3rd edn 1994).
[3] Kazuo Ishiguro, *Remains of the Day* (Faber and Faber, 1989).

Fifth, our servant (who may by now seem to be epitomised by Jeeves, the perfect servant characterised in the novels of P.G. Wodehouse) has a well-stocked mind. He's well-informed, and so is able to offer good advice. He (or she) is also able to relate unpalatable truth and has the courage to risk unpopularity in so doing. The servant certainly is not servile — nor for that matter superior — but, knowing and understanding the role of genuine service, *speaks from alongside in a relationship of both respect and trust*.

Sixth, *the servant isn't lazy*, but is hardworking, technically expert and efficient. He does not waste resources but is honest; if called to account for his behaviour, he does so willingly. There is nothing underhand here, for integrity is a key attribute of servanthood.

Seventh — we have listed some professional attributes; but since we are discussing perfection, we may want to add some personal characteristics. The servant is *witty and companionable*. We are not talking about an ice-cold automaton, but someone who inhabits our house and with whom we can have a relationship that is enjoyable as well as professional. We may want to add other qualities, such as *compassion and gentleness*; such as not *boasting*, telling you all the time how clever they are; and *courtesy*. Not formality, just appropriate courtesy — after all, I am paying him or her. And of course, *punctuality*.

Eighth, *our servant has to recognise, especially in a large family, that he or she can't do everything*. You can't be in two places at once. There are choices to make, there have to be priorities. The employing family has to understand this too and not expect everything to be done all the time. Let's root our perfection in reality.

Ninth, at the busy times when more help is needed, or if the number being served is very large, other servants will be brought in to do things which our own servant, however perfect, is not able to do. We may want to contract out some of the work to a specialist governess, pastor, chauffeur, gardener or cook, and *our own servant will be expected to work smoothly and professionally alongside such people without tantrums, jealously, or condescension*. It would be up to me as the employer to define the roles and resources with some precision, to make sure that all the servants worked well together. I may even have to ask myself the question: 'Would I get better service if I allowed all the servants in my house to compete with each other?'

Tenth — and this is tricky — my ideal of the perfect servant, however much I value his or her service and appreciate all that is done, must in the end be affordable. It is not simply a matter of providing value for money (which in any case is difficult to evaluate because it isn't like buying quantified items or even like buying a service such as gas or water). As you can see from my list this includes a number of intangibles like trust, integrity, and a relationship. Nevertheless, since I have other things to do with my money, my servant must not bankrupt me. Long-term affordability is crucial.

Now it may be that you have been relating my ten servant attributes or functions to public service broadcasting as I have gone along. If so, you will be well ahead in planning your next quarter's programme schedule! But before I catch up with you there is an essential link to make. These lectures are given within the context of Contemporary Christianity. We must therefore stop and ask ourselves: 'Do these ideas of perfect service bear any relationship to our understanding of the servanthood of Christ?' Are they just fanciful notions of today's meaning of customer service, or do they have a deeper significance; a better model; a greater authority? Only if we can regard them as being at least in part Christlike, can we apply them to broadcasting with any serious validity.

Christ as Servant-Leader

Looking at the Gospel accounts, what do we make of the matter of loyalty and single-mindedness? That is certainly Christ-like: the absence of a self-serving abuse of a position of trust or responsibility. Jesus knew what he had come to do. He didn't get sidetracked into serving other interests like power, money, or fame. In his stories and parables, and his dealing with individuals, he also understood cultural relevance and had a compassionate recognition of weaknesses in people and society. Yet he refused to condemn, although he frequently challenged people's views. He served the high and the low of his day: rulers of the Synagogue, Roman officers, beggars and prostitutes. He met people's needs for healing, psychological counsel, or food. He certainly gave advice — sometimes welcome, sometimes not — and he gave it with integrity and courage. While on earth here, Christ couldn't and didn't do everything; he had his priorities, which he often explained. As for working alongside others, he specifically trained people to carry on his work and he certainly expects us to work cooperatively with him now. The matter of cost and affordability *is* difficult. Different criteria apply. But you could say that Christ's work for us was priceless, but someone else was paying. Otherwise it would have bankrupted us.

And how did Jesus serve his people? What did he actually do for them? The Gospels show us that he taught them, explained things to them, healed them, loved them, spent time with them, challenged, questioned, rebuked them, told them stories and parables, fed them, prayed with them, gave them work to do, cried over them, defended them, washed their feet — and ultimately sacrificed himself for them.

Are these servant activities or leader activities? They are both. It's actually difficult to separate them, because when we serve someone so well that we exceed their expectations, we are in fact providing leadership; perhaps by giving them a vision of what *is* possible, and empowering them to go further next time.

The point I want to make here is that Jesus wasn't just concerned with a person's spiritual state. Out of the twenty-eight or twenty-nine encounters with individuals recorded in the New Testament (it depends how you count these things), only five were initiated on a spiritual basis. The others were to do with needs stated or unstated: for healing and well-being (physical or psychological), sexual morals, money, information, or recognition. In other words, he was and is concerned with the *whole* person. What's more he appeared more concerned about the individual than the mass. There are references to whole groups and nations, but Jesus always treated people as individuals, tailoring his thought-patterns and language to them.

I do not want to make too close an analogy between Christ's public ministry and public service broadcasting. There are obvious and clear differences between the divine nature of Christ's servant role and his authority, and any kind of service offered by radio and television. But there are enough parallels between the Christian model of perfect servanthood and the ideals of public service to allow practical application. And if we are to live our lives, and run our broadcasting Christianly, we must attempt to bring coherence to what we believe privately and what we do professionally. In doing that, we must understand the implications of Christian service for broadcasting.

Broadcasting as Servant

When people say that broadcasting in Britain is best, or among the best, in the world, I think it is because many of the servant characteristics are clearly in place. Its purpose is *not* simply to serve the powerful — neither the politically powerful, nor the commercially powerful — although both of these groups will have legitimate views to be expressed. Single-minded public service always puts the individual listener and viewer first, and recognises that this priority does not necessarily coincide with a political desire to gain popularity or persuade. Neither is there any automatic link between the ability to purchase air-time and the desire genuinely to serve the public interest. Simply because organisations or individuals have enough money to buy airtime does not mean that they have my interests at heart. Of course we should be concerned with the ownership of radio and television channels. We should not leave it simply to Channel 4's Michael Grade to protest when Rupert Murdoch's television and press interests appear to grow too powerful. A broad diversity of ownership and of programme production is a proper and necessary safeguard against overall control of the media. A certain amount of anarchy and confusion in the media — or inside any organisation within it — is essential. This dissonance of many voices, however uncomfortable it might be for some Christians, is part of the price we pay for not being subjected to a stream of well-coordinated messages from the top.

And of course we should protest when under government rules precious public facilities are sold to the highest bidder. Is money to be the arbiter of public service excellence? Are our programmes to come from whoever is the next big lottery winner? Would anyone choose a servant on grounds of finance alone? There are safeguards, of course, but in the area of public communication we must be aware of those decisions which affect such an important pipeline of our cultural water supply — and I say this about religious as well as commercial programme suppliers. So my first warning concerns the temptation of broadcasters — especially those who are the gate-keepers to airtime — to try to look in two directions at once. The true servant is not so diverted. Of course cost is important, but good service also has a proper price.

Then there is the matter of serving people in ways that meet their needs and are culturally relevant to them. This means for example that broadcasting serves as our teacher not just at school but throughout our lives. It means that programmes for our children are made very specifically for a known age range, they are based on *their* interests, values, and expectations — and provided at a time suitable to them. It also means not importing programmes from another culture simply to fill time-slots, or because a supplier has bought the time. So my second warning is about the imposition of one culture upon another. Broadcasting in Africa and Asia contains a great deal of what I would call cultural imposition — much of it for financial reasons, and a good deal of it in religious programmes. I should make it clear that I don't apply these strictures to international programming like the BBC's World Service, CNN, or VOA. These services are clearly labelled as to their origin and purpose. What does concern me are those programmes imported into an indigenous schedule which do not communicate in ways appropriate to the listener's or viewer's social understanding or values. Jesus changed his style and precision of communication very carefully to suit the person he was addressing. So should we. It is not a Christian service to treat any culture as if it were the same as mine. And this principle applies also within British society.

Continuing the Christ-like precedent, broadcasting should as far as possible try to meet the needs of the whole person (not just our entertainment and information needs). We have to treat people as individuals, not simply as a bloc — even a minority bloc — within the mass-media section. The whole person of course includes the spiritual. You hear some people these days say that regular church-going has declined to something like 10% and that interest in religion is dying. Not a bit of it! There is no logical quantitative connection between the number of people who go to church and those who recognise within themselves a spiritual need, even if it surfaces only occasionally. You might as well say that the only people interested in politics are those who go to meetings or are members of a political party, or that interest in football is confined to those who attend football matches. No, many people — most people, 73%, according to the 1990 Christian Research Association poll — recognise some kind of spiritual dimension in their lives, that the tangible here-and-now is not all there is. Sixty-five per cent of Britain's population claims a Christian adherence. It comes out most clearly in times of personal or national trauma, in the aftermath of disastrous or tragic circumstances; in bereavement for example. (The

Oklahoma bombing illustrates this only too well.) People flock to churches, they pray to God when they don't know where else to turn. This need in human beings exists, but since churches are obviously not meeting it fully, what about the broadcasters? Yes, there are many excellent counselling and help programmes, especially on local radio and daytime television, which don't treat people who have real questions and problems simply as microphone fodder and sometimes as objects of voyeuristic ridicule. Programmes can and do respond with unpatronising responsibility. They are often not religious programmes in any sense; but I would nevertheless regard them as Christ-like, in that they treat people as individuals and set out to meet their needs.

I think we can take some pride in this country in being unique (I believe I am right in saying this) in that our national instrument of broadcasting, the BBC, has broadcast an act of worship of some kind every day since its inception in 1922. Those of us who want to live by our faith in everything, and not just keep God for emergencies, would want to say 'long may it remain so'. But in these more competitive times even this area seems under threat. To me this would be as odd as threatening to relegate the time available for politics or football. My third warning therefore is that deciding not to meet the needs of the whole person by leaving out the spiritual dimension (which, as I have said, the great majority recognises) would be of course a serious form of bias — not to say censorship. It would represent a lack of balance every bit as bad as saying we will only reflect government views and not opposition ones. To reflect only the material world and not the spiritual would be a quite unjustifiable decision for any servant to take. However, these questions will be addressed more fully in a later lecture.

An aspect of service which I have raised a number of times is to do with the relationship between the provider and the consumer. It is implicit in such words as compassion, integrity, and trust. Anyway the word 'communication' means sharing, not telling. Broadcasting has in the past been somewhat arrogant; some of it still is. But I'm glad to say it is changing and trying to develop a warmer, more useful relationship with the listener and viewer. It is doing this by offering more 'after-sales' care in the form of supplementary information, scripts for sale, and help-lines. It is not enough simply to provide programmes on a take-it-or-leave-it basis. Service means providing access to broadcasters, to ask and answer questions, to allow for complaint, for personal redress, to publish reaction to programmes, or comment on the programme company or station. There are public meetings and station open days, and audience research and programme panels to identify both needs and results.

I would like to think that this increased contact between broadcaster and audience stemmed from the God-given principle that good communication is essentially relational. However I think it is much more due to increased competition — the clamour for attention. Nevertheless the end result is likely to be the same so long as we remember that there are deeper reasons why public service broadcasting must become more relational still.

What else from our servant models can we apply to broadcasting? A well-stocked mind, properly informed and responsible as opposed to sensational, inaccurate, and incompetent. We asked our domestic servant to be witty and companionable, as well as having the courage to be on occasion unpopular. A friend whom I really trust does not humiliate or embarrass me yet has the right to tell me things I don't like; I give him, or allow him, that right. But what about broadcasters obsessed with being popular — do *they* have that right? They are unelected, they have no mandate to steer public opinion in one direction or another; any kind of social engineering or covert persuasion is strictly out. But that doesn't mean that the voice of protest or radicalism is not heard, that warnings are not given.

Broadcasting as a Reflector of Right and Wrong

I think the best newspaper *title* we have is the *Daily Mirror*. A perfect mirror truly reflects what is going on in society. It shows us without distortion who we are, what we are doing, and what we are thinking. It does not leave bits out or emphasise particular areas. It truly represents the whole picture. So genuine independence should mean that broadcasters do not lobby me from a particular viewpoint about say, euthanasia, animal welfare, or European politics, but that I hear the whole story — both sides, or as many sides as necessary to reflect as many views as necessary, adequately expressed — in order to help me make up my own mind.

So do the media represent a perfectly reflecting mirror of society? Of course not. Their greatest distortion is that they are highly selective in what they choose to present. The News is not about normality, but abnormality. Drama has more incident, danger, murder, and love affairs than there have ever been in my own life. I've had adventure and crises in my own family, but not, I'm glad to say, at the required rate of three every fifteen minutes. Conflict and its resolution is the very stuff of story-telling, and always has been; there's nothing new in that. Jane Austen's gentle *Pride and Prejudice* is an account of the class tensions and private manners of middle-class life in southern England in the 1820s. But it is a concentrated account, a distillation, partial and selective to make its points. You see, we the audience say something very loudly to books, films, and programmes: 'Interest me!' So they leave out the humdrum, the everyday, and the boring. They concentrate on the feelings and events that drive the story on — the juicy bits. As of course does the Bible.

The Gospels tell us about Jesus' life, but very little indeed about his first thirty years. We have some of his activities and teaching as an itinerant preacher, and most of all about his last few days on earth. But if you add up the total elapsed time about which we have any information about his three-year ministry, I doubt you'd have a week and a half — less than 1%. If you've ever asked yourself what the Gospel of John has in common with *Match of the Day*, there it is: the highlights. Selective, concentrated, the most interesting; the most important, the memorable bits. And yes, that's a distortion in the sense that it isn't the whole — it just has to represent it. So when people ask 'Why is there so much sex and violence and bad news on the media?', that's part of the answer. The medium distorts by compression and selective exaggeration. The interesting thing about the whole truth is that the whole truth isn't interesting.

Now, I don't want a servant to tell me what I should do, much less what I should think. However, he can provide me with options so that if I have a need to come to a conclusion about something, my perfect, unbiased, well-informed servant can help me. Again, we have a Christ-like characteristic here. Jesus so often told a story, a parable, without tying up all the loose ends. Sometimes he gave advice in answer to a question and then let the person walk away. In the end, everything he said and did was apparently rejected. Would we be willing to listen to, or watch, and in one way or another pay for, a service which many of us might want to reject — particularly if we don't much like being troubled by difficult issues? This question brings us to the contentious area of finance — of being affordable.

Money as a Secondary Concern

The first thing is this. Money is important, the servant mustn't bankrupt me — but it's not the most important thing. It doesn't matter how cheap or how affordable a service may be (it might even be apparently 'free' — financed by the State) but if I don't trust it, it is worthless. As with religion, believability is more important than cost.

The second point has to do with the much discussed areas of value for money, and efficiency. The managements of organisations today are increasingly scrutinised for their operating efficiency and ability to produce as much as possible for their money. This is especially important when it's public money. But organisations cannot be 100% efficient — and neither do I want them to be. I do not want a hospital, for example, to be used 100%; I want it to have spare unused capacity so that it can cope properly with emergencies. The margin between average usage and total capacity is a form of insurance. I use some of my personal resources for insurance and for the most part it is quite unproductive. Fortunately I rarely claim the benefits of my investment in insurance. In that sense it is inefficient. The same principle should be applied to public finance.

Let me explain what in my opinion justifies radio and television working at less than 100% efficiency. The creative process of programme-making as we know requires ideas to be explored which may not see the light of day. The search for quality demands some trial and error. We have to experiment, to have the freedom to make mistakes; not all initial scripts or film will end up on air or on the screen. So how are we to trust the broadcasters not to waste or misuse the money they receive from us by advertising, subscription, or licence?

Remember, I'm arguing from the position that the primary concern of public service broadcasting is to serve the audience, not to make money. I will pay my domestic servant but (and this may come as a strange notion to some) it is not the first concern of those who are called to serve to accumulate wealth. It is a matter of primary motivation. So my answer about financial efficiency is that given proper accountability, we must trust them. The basis for financial integrity is the same as for news reporting, documentary programmes, or for that matter drama, education, or light entertainment.

And how is such trust to be gained? We come back to the Christian values to which I referred earlier: the 'Christianness' of both leadership and servanthood depends on a recognised relationship. It is the relation between the broadcaster on the one hand and the listener and viewer on the other which underpins both programme believeability and financial trust. As I have said, without trust broadcasting — or any form of communication — is worth nothing, as totalitarian regimes eventually discover.

The Leader Role

We have so far been concentrating on the servant role of broadcasting. Let me turn now to its function as a leader, and consider how the two might be integrated.

Leadership is simpler than servanthood; not easier, just simpler. I want to describe it in just two dimensions. If I am going to lead I must know where I am going, so the first requirement of leadership is *vision*. Without vision, says Proverbs, the people perish, or fall apart. Certainly the biblical basis for the Christian faith is full of visionary statements — clear propositions of purpose, of 'what ifs', and pictures of how the future could be. In fact this is part of the service which faith offers.

But is broadcasting doing this? It tends to wallow somewhat in anniversary nostalgia, to react to current events and speculate in short-term futures. But this is not what I mean. Do enough programmes of all types extrapolate trends to describe possible longer-term futures? Are we sufficiently forward-looking in our media? It is not necessarily the job of radio and television to take us there, but the first dimension of leadership is to point out various ways, leading to possible destinations; painting pictures of how things might be, sounding warnings if need be — at least asking questions on our behalf.

The second dimension of leadership is the *empowerment* of people to succeed in times of transition and change. 'Empowerment' is often thought to be part of modern management jargon, but the idea is at least 2,000 years old: Jesus spoke of the empowerment of the coming Holy Spirit. Here I simply mean that broadcasting has a role in preparing and training people to come to terms with new ideas and visions: new technologies like computers, e-mail, the Internet; facing the fears and opportunities of new medical practices; questioning new political realities of Europe; new economics; the future needs for employment and unemployment, for wealth or poverty, for education and training. Certainly *something* is being done. We might get a programme about Euro-currency, or on ILR's Metro about the non-future of the north-east's shipyards. But out of the thousands of hours of output, is it enough? It is far easier to run a film or play a record to satisfy in the short-term, and this as I have indicated is a serious trend throughout the industry.

Trends and Directions

Short-termism may pass as leadership because it looks decisive, but it lacks vision, it's not strategic. It is counterfeit: at best pragmatism, at worst expediency. Alvin Toffler in *Future Shock*[4] drew attention to our increasingly short-term world. With news on the hour and the half hour, the pressure is always to report new news — that is, what's happened in the last half hour. We become obsessed with short events, with facts rather than process. We are interested in the 'what', 'when' and 'where', rather than the 'how' and 'why'. Journalism, especially competitive journalism, is essentially about the short-term; and as that affects our output so it affects us internally as well. Journalistic organisations, by their very reactive nature, find it difficult to think strategically. There is an unwillingness to invest in the long term. We have short-term contracts, which in turn reduces training opportunities. We have managers on such contracts, so why should they care about the long-term development of their people? Why should they bother about annual appraisal? And without other people caring about my work and what I do, I may eventually get the feeling myself that it doesn't matter. It's just noises, pictures in the air; ephemeral, short-lived, and lacking in any real significance. Is that what we want?

In 1987 I carried out a study in the BBC. I asked 50 senior managers, two-thirds of them men and one-third women, what it was that most enabled them to progress. To what did they attribute their success — their significance? Was it their super-competence? Some special training they'd had? A job opportunity that came up? None of these. Two-thirds of the men and slightly more of the women attributed their break to the intervention of a senior person.

---
[4] Alvin Toffler, *Future Shock* (Bodley Head, 1970).

Someone else had said, 'You should take a regional attachment,' or 'I want you to be part of a special project.' In other words, someone with a longer view of the future had encouraged a career move. The typical age for this change of key was between 34 and 37. So for the group I was looking at in their late forties and fifties, this had happened some twenty years earlier, say in 1968–70. Does this happen today? I hope so, but somehow I doubt it. I understand that in any case less than 2% of BBC staff today are over 50. The people with longer-term experience and commitment have gone. Is it the same elsewhere? I think so. The industry is much more mobile than it was, and I understand the reasons for this. But — and this is my fourth warning — at a time when we talk more than ever about strategy, actual personal commitment to long-term vision, especially in individual leadership, seems in short supply. And I think this is serious.

Another area in which we don't invest so readily in the long-term is that of our operational technology. The problem is that development is so rapid, new equipment may soon be out of date. Rather than buy, it is easier to contract out.

Unconsciously perhaps, short-termism affects our staff relations, the way we deal with each other, and our programme and financial planning. Pragmatism rules. Political expediency is too easily the order of the day. It contrasts pointedly with real leadership, which depends on vision. It is the opposite end of the spectrum from religious faith which, while it is concerned with the day to day, never loses sight of the eternal. Perhaps once again money is at the root of it. If we are never quite sure of our licence fee or our franchise, we will tend to play safe. The long-term is risky.

And what are the other current trends which may impede either genuine service or true leadership? I mentioned short-term contracts. Let me return for a moment to my perfect domestic servant. He or she has to have reasonable tenure of employment — a salaried position — otherwise he is likely to spend too much time looking out for other possibilities, worried about where the next job is coming from. Mind you, a lot of people with a freelance mindset like living off tips and commission — it keeps them on their mettle, helping to promote a flow of energetic ideas. It certainly affects the way you work. The counter-argument is that too much security may breed complacency. Yes this is possibly the case, but not with a vigilant employer.

The point I want to make — and my next warning — is, that it seems oddly undermining to have alongside the freelance market, an institution like the BBC which itself decides to operate a series of internal markets and in effect treat its staff also like freelances under instructions to break even. As some people prefer to work vicariously, so some will do their best work within an organisational security. But this is disappearing as the public sector behaves as if it is being privatised. Yet our British system has thrived on *complementary* ways of working. Different methods of financing, different scheduling and operating procedures have often been given as the key reason why our separate practices are able to coexist so well within the broadcasting ecology. So, warning number five: there are dangers in creating market-place similarities throughout the whole industry, especially when because of the licence fee the BBC does not need deliberately to copy everyone else. Let distinctive kinds of programme emerge from different methods of funding.

Another trend, one which is affecting local broadcasting — both in ILR and in BBC stations — is their amalgamation, either through company merger or what the BBC has referred to as 'rational integration'. I have to warn (and this is my sixth and last warning) that it will fail. If we are not careful we shall be re-inventing the old Regions, which would entirely defeat the purpose of creating a local sense of identity. The best listening figures have always come from those places with the strongest sense of community. Making programmes for too wide an audience — geographically or culturally — is likely to end up pleasing no one. Broadcasting organisations cannot dictate where the 'boundaries of belonging' will run. As I have said, we have to recognise that the servant can't do everything. The suspicion here is that the BBC and ILR want a comprehensive national news presence, without giving a proper service in return.

So there are the six warnings, or at least concerns, that I have about current directions in broadcasting. I have warned that the pursuit of value for money may become simply a search for ways of lowering costs; that programme syndication is too often seen as a good thing irrespective of cultural relevance; that deliberately reducing the religious dimension is a form of censorship; that there is little incentive for today's broadcasting managers to be long-term strategic visionaries; that British broadcasting is constrained by a market-driven mindset which overlooks the distinctive advantage of the licence fee; and that another kind of distinctiveness is under threat, as local broadcasters amalgamate into ever-larger regions.

The Media We Deserve?

The sub-title of this lecture series, 'The Word on the Box', is: 'Do we get the media we deserve?' I hope that each of the speakers will attempt to answer this, but since I'm first, I think that I at least should try to! Do we get the media we deserve? Yes, I think we do. The media are certainly not worse than we deserve, and in some ways are a good deal better. We live in a fallen world — the heart of man is essentially wicked, says the Bible. We are preoccupied with self, which on a personal level leads to selfish pride, competitive status, acquisitive gain, sexual promiscuity, and conflict. On a national level this so often becomes nationalistic aggrandisement to the extent of hating others. Xenophobia between cultures is all too common.

So if we are so interested in sex and violence (and we are) we can hardly complain that the media give it to us. If they did not, we would accuse them either of being out of touch with reality, or of exercising a puritanical censorship for which they had no right. It is part of being the mirror which I referred to earlier; society, good and bad, being reflected back to us. It is quite unquestionable that such matters are a legitimate part of society's communication to itself. The issue is always about where precisely to draw the line. And this is difficult, because it varies greatly from individual to individual. If for me the line is drawn too soon, too discreetly, I will say, 'Come on, how pathetic! What are we *not* seeing or hearing?' — and that applies to news reporting from a disaster, just as much as to drama. If the line is drawn too late then my reaction will be of offence: 'How coarse, or vulgar!' Or, 'Don't treat me like an idiot — I do have *some* imagination.' It's the endless question for producers — how to have impact without smashing the listener or viewer in the face. I think radio is the more subtle medium here. It is more suggestive without being explicit, because it is so visual. Of course I don't expect radio or television always to get it right for me. How could they? It is my preferences we are talking about. We must take a broad view, that other people have different preferences. Have you noticed that in discussions of programme standards people talk as though the danger is always of other people being corrupted — never themselves? I say again: in God's eyes, we are all corrupted. For the most part, the line is drawn where I want it to be because it is self-regulating. As a listener or viewer the ultimate sanction — the off-switch or channel button — is mine. If I do not wish to have what I regard as the licentious or tawdry, the ugly or demeaning (and there are such programmes) then no one compels me to have it. It is a matter of choice.

So what did I mean by saying that the media are sometimes better than we deserve? Simply that on occasion one becomes part of something so inspiring, intriguing, forceful, or beautiful, that it is an experience which takes you out of the everyday into the realms of the very special. We have the country's best performers, writers, reporters, sportsmen and women and presenters doing this for us every day; and sometimes they succeed hugely. I won't give you a long list of what I mean, it's personal and we each have our own list. But let me just mention one by way of illustration.

BBC Radio 4 did a 1995 anniversary programme; a drama documentary called 'Bomber', it was about a wartime bomber raid over Germany, but it was done in real time in chunks over an afternoon and evening — from the initial briefing, the take-off, the flight, the raid (by which time everything had gone horribly wrong); and it was all interwoven with the personal details of the people in the air and on the ground on both sides, together with the actuality and voices of the people who had done this for real, fifty years before. It was immensely complex. You had to stay up until midnight to hear the planes — some of them — returning home. Anguish, death, hope, bewildering despair — it was innovative as well as authentic; and it was terrific radio. There are many others, of course. I enjoy much of what I see and hear. But are such personal highpoints servant or leader? Well they are both. They meet unsuspected needs so providing a service, but they also exercise leadership in creatively taking me somewhere I've not been before.

A Christian Response

Finally, let me address the future from a Christian standpoint. And within the present context I mean by that, developing the public service nature of our broadcasting so that it is more relational and provides both service and leadership. In Britain today this means meeting a wide range of needs within a culturally complex pluralistic society comprising many minorities, and providing for that society both vision and empowerment to help people cope with change.

First we need to encourage the debate — of which this series of lectures is a part. Too much talk of radio and television is as I have indicated, about individual programmes; about sex, violence, and bad language — yes, and about excellence, about superb artistry, writing and design. All that is necessary and desirable, but there is not nearly enough about the medium itself and how it is changing our lives.

We look back at the invention of print and realise its hugely important role in transferring power from those few who could read and write (the State, the Church, and the Law) to the great mass of the people. The social significance of printing for civilisation is more than the impact of any one book. So what is broadcasting actually doing in speeding up the dissemination of information worldwide and the sharing of cultural values? On balance, does it stimulate, inform us, challenge, and warn, or does it pass the time, lulling us to sleep in the warm soapy waters of the uninvolving sit-com? We need a bit of both. But from what I have said, there is no doubt in my own mind where, Christianly, the balance should be.

I welcome the initiative of organisations like the Jerusalem Trust and the Media Awareness Project, in holding seminars to discuss these issues. We have to look at the long term to provide an antidote, or at least a balance, to pragmatic short-termism — and risk being called starry-eyed idealists in the process. It's very important for Christians to be involved in the huge changes which are coming in the whole process of public communication. There has been a feeling that the media are somehow un-Christian, even that they are the work of the devil, or at least too much to do with the secular world as to be unworthy of Christian involvement. I have met such extreme views; in fact Malcolm Muggeridge seemed very much in that camp. But I have to remind us that the opposite of 'spiritual' is not 'secular' but 'profane'. The secular world is very much the place we inhabit. So why aren't the churches or their agents more involved in programme production? Why isn't there a stronger Christian voice on contemporary issues? It's important for Christians to be making programmes — and I don't just mean religious programmes. This church, St Peter's Vere Street, is home to the Arts Centre Group which fosters and encourages Christians who are professional artists of all kinds. So where are our Christian dramatists and writers? Are there enough as media opportunities increase? Their world view on all issues is an essential component among all the other voices which we hear. I welcome Premier Radio in London as a source of Christian commentary. It is part of the proliferation of stations and channels — but, let us note, an expansion that is leading to broadcasting's own decline in importance. As there are more and more programmes, as digital audio gives us more channels, as direct broadcasting by satellite rains them down from the sky from any part of the world, and as cable provides CD-ROM libraries, and computer games, databases, and networks into our home — so each programme has less and less impact, is less and less important.

We want broadcasters to be concerned with the immeasurable as well as the measurable. Money and audience ratings are important and my colleagues in this series will expand on these. But the other things I have mentioned like believability, trust, integrity and affection are even more crucial; for without them there is no communication — and the reason for this truth lies at the heart of the biblical gospel.

In Genesis 1, God says 'Let us make man in our image.' 'Let *us* . . . *our* image.' God already lives within a relationship of Father, Son, and Holy Spirit. We are in that same mould — essentially relational. Men and women are relational beings: so must our broadcasting be, both in our programmes and increasingly in their follow-up. Broadcasting is not just a business. Certainly there are business aspects to it, for our agreements require clarity, there needs to be precision in our planning and professionalism in our standards. We have to be business-like. But human communication also, and essentially, requires compassion, tolerance, truth, warmth, and humour. What's more, you can't broadcast these things to an audience unless they already exist within the industry. It is a good exercise to write down those things that you want to be for your audience, those characteristics you would like to have come over: and then to ask, 'But do they first exist as values here within our production company, station, programme department, or corporation?' We are unlikely to be something to others unless we first behave in that way to each other.

In short, communication is God's own business. He cares about good communication and detests lies, falsehood, malice, and slander. In fact it is the Devil who is described as 'the deceiver' and the father of lies. John's Gospel speaks of the Word being made flesh and dwelling among us. As Colin Morris [5] has observed, broadcasting is so often simply the flesh being made word (and, let me add, not dwelling among us). Too much radio and television in the past has felt élitist and out of touch. It suffered from a sense of self-importance, perhaps brought about by its grandiose technology or an assumed status as society's mouthpiece. Well, it is no longer special. There is too much competition for that, and as for the technology, the camcorder makes everyone their own director, and the video our own scheduler. Yes, broadcasting is even more now the servant in our very household.

But of course, the best place from which to communicate is not as our servant, nor from somewhere up ahead as our leader. Much more effective is to be alongside, and this is surely what 'dwelling among us' means — communicating in ways that are personally or at least culturally relevant. God's messengers have always brought the news of his love for us in terms which underline and sustain our *significance* and our *security*; and broadcasting should do the same. And in case you think that finally my visions of perfection have at last overcome the real world, let me recall a local radio station where listeners sent Christmas cards thanking the station (i) for being a good friend, (ii) for putting their city on the map, and (iii) helping so much in times of emergency. You can hardly better that! Relational broadcasting which offers people a sense of security, significance and service. That's God's work — the servant and the leader. No I'm not talking just about religious programmes, and I'm not even talking about Christian broadcasting. But I am talking about broadcasting Christianly.

---

[5] Rev. Colin Morris is former Head of BBC Religious Broadcasting, and Controller Northern Ireland.

2: Is More News Good News?

Justin Phillips

To a broadcast journalist, this title will seem a very strange one, for most journalists would immediately respond, 'Of course! The more news the better!'

After all, news is the very air we breathe, and a journalist can no more survive without it than a fish can without water. Even on holiday we journalists find it hard to switch off. One of the first things I do when abroad is to tune my short-wave radio receiver into the BBC World Service and find a shop where I can buy a paper. Then, my news 'fix' assured, I can relax. Once one of the many Jerusalem-based news correspondents went on holiday to Cyprus and left his short-wave radio behind. It took two days for his news organisation to track him down. By then his two radio-free days on the beach meant that he had missed one-third of the Six Day War! With head hung low, he managed to scramble back to Jerusalem before it was all over. He's never been without his radio since.

It's getting very hard to escape from news today. Even listeners to classical music, who in the past have had their news well-spaced and enjoyed a relatively news-free zone in the mornings now have to hear their Tchaikovsky alongside traffic reports and their Wagner woven around the weather forecast. But, as one Norwegian journalist once told me, to a journalist news is the meaning of life.

Even if we journalists like to live in our own virtual reality bubble, eating, drinking and sleeping news, our readers, listeners and viewers may take a rather different view. But without doubt there is a huge appetite for news. And whether we like it or not, in the next five years we are going to see more and more news available through more and more outlets. Not just via the medium of radio and television and that precious antiquity the printed page, but also via cable, teletext, satellite, and on-line services from video-on-demand to news icons on our PC. News is growing at a faster rate than ever before. It has become an ever expanding universe, with its bright stars, its swirling galaxies, its clouds of gas and air (though it undeniably has its share of black holes as well). The variety of news available on British radio alone is already becoming very impressive.

The more traditional news and current affairs programmes have maintained their audiences in the face of this new competition. Radio 4's *Today*, where I was a producer in the era of Brian Redhead and John Timpson, remains the nation's most popular speech programme on radio. More people prefer to hear their news on radio in the mornings than to watch it on breakfast television. The television news audience comes into its own at night with the BBC and ITN still enjoying their traditional dogfight between news at nine o'clock on BBC1 and at ten on ITV. Into this equation must be added new arrivals on radio and television, on satellite, cable and on other electronic media. You can hear the news in so many different formats now, and on stations that focus on talk radio or use a video-format to turn news round more quickly. Internet users can keep up to date with headlines and news, and select audio clips and pictures. Digital Audio Broadcasting offers continuous news and information updates. The variations and the diversity continue to expand at a breathtaking rate, not to mention other news media such as newspapers.

Among the many changes that have taken place is the fundamental one of the core relationship between the news provider and those who watch and listen to broadcast news. As choice multiplies, the audience has more say and more control. To that extent we all receive the media we deserve and broadcast the news that our audience demands. With so many stations to choose between and so many media, the listener and viewer can choose. No one *has* to listen to the BBC any more, not even those who work for it. Broadcasters can take nothing for granted.

Robert McLeish's vision of the public broadcaster as servant and as leader is one with which the Christian can readily identify. I want to build on that to focus specifically on my area of expertise, which is that of broadcast news, and to examine some of the changes taking place and the implications for us. Then I want to suggest a distinctive Christian approach: the role of the news provider to inform with truth and integrity. We will then explore some of the real dangers

Is More News Good News? 25

and pitfalls that lie ahead alongside the opportunities being created in this new world information order.

Inevitably, much of what I say will be informed by an insider's awareness of developments taking place within our industry; but what I have to say here is a purely personal view. These are my own thoughts and do not in any way purport to represent those of the BBC, my employer. This is a look at news broadcasting as a whole, not what is happening in the BBC. I shall attempt to answer some questions, many put to me at talks and lectures given to media students, school pupils and church members. How should we respond to the changes and growth taking place in broadcast news as journalists, as Christians, as viewers and listeners? Is the exponential growth of news a glimpse of heaven or a return to the Tower of Babel? Do we embrace it, applaud it, deplore it or just ignore it? We certainly cannot avoid it.

My approach is fourfold. First, to identify the driving forces behind the growth in news availability — this puts the whole debate into context. Then to suggest a Christian approach to help us respond to these changes. Next I shall outline the risks and the dangers news proliferation is bringing, and I will end by underlining the opportunities this also brings.

THE DRIVING FORCES

Competition

When I began my broadcasting career in 1973 with LBC (London Broadcasting, Britain's first commercial radio station), Londoners had a choice of seven domestic radio stations: four BBC national networks, BBC Radio London, LBC and Capital Radio. By 1991, the choice for Londoners was even greater. LBC and Capital had split frequencies, with Capital Gold playing oldies on the AM frequency. London Talkback held sway on medium wave with LBC Newstalk on FM. Add to this four new specialist stations: Spectrum offering an ethnic music mix, Kiss offering dance music, Jazz FM offering jazz and soul, and Melody playing middle-of-the road lighter music.

Five years later in 1996 the picture today is very different and much more crowded. Londoners can now choose from twenty-four national and local radio stations. Many are 'niche' broadcasters, providing specific and specialist stations for a limited but devoted radio audience. In the course of 1995, more stations added their distinctive sounds to the radio spectrum. Viva! offered talk and music just for women, but struggled to find listeners. Premier Radio was launched as London's first Christian independent commercial station. They joined a diverse rich mix of niche broadcasters in London, which includes London Greek Radio and Spectrum Radio, providing a few hours for each of London's ethnic communities; and specialist music stations like Melody, Kiss, JFM and the Country music station. Each of these provides some kind of news service, largely through hourly news summaries. Add to this Virgin and Heart with more adult-orientated rock, national Classic FM and Talk UK, and you have the most competitive radio marketplace in the UK.

In Britain as a whole, competition is fierce and intense. The number of commercial radio services has grown from 16 to more than 170 over the past twenty years. In the last decade, the rate of expansion accelerated from this combination of frequency splits, new licences and the launch of independent national radio. This meant, too, that that the number of services available to a listener has risen rapidly. This increase in competition has put pressure on both the BBC and commercial radio to compete for a share of that audience, and to reach as many listeners tuning in for a measurable period as possible.

Astonishingly, some estimates suggest that the number of commercial radio stations could rise even further. If community radio takes off, we could see over 200 new stations broadcasting at a very local level on top of additional stations licensed by the Radio Authority. Add these together and you could be talking about nearly 400 commercial stations within the next decade. But it's not just the choice that will increase. So will the different ways we use our radios and technology to receive news services.

I'm not exaggerating unduly when I say that until recently, it was the news broadcasters who decided when and how our audiences would receive the news. We, the broadcasters, used to decide when news was made available. Like the children of Israel at the foot of Mount Sinai, waiting for Moses to come down and read out the Ten Commandments, the audience had to wait until the next scheduled news broadcast to discover what was going on in the world. Much of what we news-providers did and how we did it was shrouded in mystery. The broadcasters were in control.

What changed it all was the arrival of commercial radio, and, more recently still, twenty-four hour news. Now listeners have a choice of stations where they can hear news when they want it, not just when we the broadcasters decide to deliver. With the advent of Sky News and Radio 5 Live, news became available across the nation twenty-four hours a day. And what has been happening in domestic radio in Britain is a mirror of what has been happening on a much wider scale.

Global news growth

What has been happening in radio driven by commercial forces is also happening in television. But here the competition is being worked out on a global stage with big money at stake. In different media, different alliances are emerging. You have only to read the media pages to see them take shape. If I were to list them here, that list would be out of date before the printer's ink had dried. The editorial values vary from organisation to organisation. Inevitably, the quality and range of coverage will be in direct proportion to the resources that broadcaster has invested into news gathering. When CNN began, many observers felt that its coverage, though impartial, reflected an American world view. Coverage of events in countries like the Philippines, Korea and Central America seemed more likely to crop up than coverage of Spain or Norway or Zaire. But as CNN has developed and expanded, its news coverage has become more international, remained impartial and gained in credibility.

Many of the biggest names in broadcasting and publishing from British Telecom to Time Warner, from Microsoft to Pearson and Reuters, ITN and the BBC, are all looking at new ways to deliver news. What we are seeing is not just the arrival of the global media player, but a huge growth in the number of ways that the news product can be delivered.

Rupert Murdoch of News International told the BBC's *Money Programme* (21 May 1995):

> In terms of the information highway working and delivering by fibre-optics into every home in the world or by satellite, I think that it's several years, five years, before you see the completion of the fibre-optic network in America; and in Britain and in Europe, that's at least 15 years

away .... We are sailing blind in a way. What we're saying is, there are so many options open that we'd better have options for ourselves, and that's why we cannot confine ourselves to being newspaper publishers, or just to television, or terrestrial television, or to pay-television or whatever it is .... We have to make sure that we have access to all the different delivery systems that are emerging.

Since this lecture was delivered on 15 May 1995 the BBC has launched its blueprint for the future in a document called 'Extending Choice in the Digital Age'. This sets out the BBC's response to the digital age. The document says that:

> Over the next 10 years and beyond, the BBC aims to seize the opportunities — and meet the challenges — offered by the digital age. We will apply digital technology, allied to the creative talents of our programme makers, to enhance and extend our existing services, and to develop distinctive, new ways of responding to the needs and interests of our audiences.

The BBC will make use of digital technology to improve its package of television services for the licence fee payer. Built around BBC1 and BBC2, the package will offer,

- wide screen digital pictures and top quality sound
- digital BBC1 and BBC2 plus optional extra services
- news available at all times. [1]

Cross-media ownership is very much a live issue and, in Britain at least, regulations exist to keep the size of any one group within clear limits while allowing more cross-media ownership. What nobody wants is for any single media conglomerate to have a controlling interest across different media. In the case of News International, Rupert Murdoch (at the time of writing) owns several national UK papers including *The Times* and the *Sun* and has a 40% stake in British Sky Broadcasting. He is active in Asia, Europe and the United States. As one commentator put it, the sun never sets on News International's empire. But in an expanding media playing-field, the teams are still being formed and reformed. New alliances are being formed, and national players are stepping onto the global stage. It is impossible to say who will forge a partnership with whom at this stage. A dozen or so major players all see a global news market opening up, and each of them wants their slice of the pie.

Some of these players are strong on delivery systems but weak on

---

[1] BBC, 'Extending Choice in the Digital Age' (June 1996).

end product; with others it is the other way round. Inevitably, we will see different companies combining their skills to work together. Barely a week goes by without new announcements of new partnerships. Here are just a few examples of some significant developments.

Polygram, the music and film producer majority-owned by the Dutch electronics group Philips, has formed a partnership with MTV, the American all-music channel. They plan a joint venture that will broadcast two music channels to the entire Asian market. MTV Mandarin and MTV Asia will get Western music across the bamboo curtain, and of course the other way round too. Will we soon be rushing out to buy the latest album by Jacky Cheung — China's Elton John?

By June 1995, Compaq was selling in Britain a personal computer with a built-in television tuner. It is now possible to watch TV while using your PC at home, or to have it running in a small section of the computer screen so you can keep abreast of Eastenders while you fill in your tax return.

Apple market a computer CDTV which combines computer, high-resolution colour screen, stereo loudspeakers, a CD-Rom drive and built-in TV tuner capable of displaying Nicam stereo broadcasts, teletext and video inputs from a camcorder or video recorder. Users can watch a movie or listen to a CD while working on home accounts. This all-singing, all-dancing technology could be the way of the future, combining in one unit all the multimedia and interactive functions you can think of.

Shopping by computer is well-established. You can now order your shopping from Sainsbury or Tesco at home via the Internet or use the net to buy chocolates from Belgium, wine from France or even elephant collectibles from a shop in Florida. Home shopping is just one of many on-line services — including news — that many think will become very popular.

The Mirror Group's Live TV has tried to make its cable TV news more lively and accessible with a 'News Bunny' that reflects sadness or joy as stories are read out. The bunny fits into its remit to offer news that is 'fast, fun, pacey and packed' with lots of celebrity stories. This is the tabloid newspaper approach, translated to cable TV and receiving a mixed reaction.

ARK2 promises a range of programmes from a Christian perspective, including material to help schools with religious education and daily worship. Both L!ve TV and ARK2 are starting from the premise that Britain's million or so cable households will grow to five or six million by the end of the century.

We have seen a series of mega takeovers and mergers. These include Disney buying ABC; MCI buying a stake in News Corporation; Microsoft going into partnership with NBC to develop a twenty-four hour news and information channel; and Viacom acquiring Paramount and Blockbuster Entertainment.

So where does all this leave the older broadcast news suppliers like the BBC and ITN? The traditional news opponents remain with horns locked, but they cannot ignore the new kids on the block, already a force to be reckoned with. We already have round-the-clock news on radio available in Britain. We have twenty-four-hour television news available on satellite and cable. It is significant that in his launch of the BBC's digital plans, John Birt included a Continuous TV News service on the BBC.

Players are joining the news merry-go-round all the time. Channel One Television is a London cable channel owned by Associated Newspapers and already available via cable to some 400,000 Londoners. It employs video journalists who submit video tape rushes which are edited digitally and ready for transmission. The gap between recording and transmission can be as little as ninety seconds. The catch-line of Channel One Television is 'News You Can Use'.

One of the BBC's commercial partners is the Pearson Group, whose holdings include the *Financial Times*. Pearson continue to expand, acquiring in 1995 Grundy International whose cultural legacy to the twentieth century includes *Neighbours* and *Prisoner Cell Block H*. The licence to run Channel 5 has been awarded to Pearson (who also own Thames TV), MAI (which controls Anglia and Meridian) and partners.

We will doubtless see more companies joining the merry-go-round. Microsoft are a world leader in personal computers. With the launch of Windows 95 and its new software packages with access to the Internet, the addition of a news service to such software has arrived. Broadcasting is being redefined by the day. In this new broadcasting environment, it is impossible to tell who will be working in competition or in partnership with whom ten years from now. It may even happen that two media organisations will work together in one field (for example, satellite broadcasting) while competing in another (such as video on demand).

In the coming years we will see all kind of alliances and competition emerging. There is so much to play for on an international media stage. The outlets are proliferating at frightening speed, as are the delivery systems. With the commercial sector funding so much of the development, public service broadcasters across the globe will have to think carefully what services and what level of involvement is possible.

In the words of American songwriter Johnny Nash, 'There are more questions than answers.' Anyone trying to predict what broadcasting will be like ten years from now can be certain only of one thing: whatever they predict will almost certainly be proved wrong!

Finance pressures: Rising costs

The harsh reality of finance is that for many broadcasters a gap is opening up between income, whether it be license fee or advertising, and spending. Many broadcasting organisation in the public sector and in commercial areas are having to make some tough choices. Often the question being faced is how to make the biggest savings with the least possible impact on air, to fund a project? We are all learning to live within tighter budgets and having to decide 'which gain for least pain'. Getting best value for money has become the order of the day.

The squeeze is on both the public service broadcasters and many in the commercial sector. Financial pressures are growing and this cuts both ways. The internal costs within radio and television are growing. Costs are going up. New technology may make possible some productivity savings, but costs are rising and at a faster rate than inflation.

Two factors forcing up internal costs are the cost of retaining top talent and the high cost of securing rights to major sporting events. Whether it is cricket or tennis, rugby or soccer, snooker, athletics or boxing, the competition is fierce. What is good news for the sport is not always good news for viewers and listeners. What impact does the creation of a World Super League in a sport like Rugby League have on the fans who want to watch it? Does it sell satellite dishes? Since this lecture was delivered, Parliament has passed the Broadcasting Act which protects a handful of listed sporting events (like the FA Cup Final and Wimbledon) and ensures that terrestrial television viewers still have access to these major events, whatever rights are bought by satellite and cable TV companies. But there are unprotected events that didn't make the list.

Although broadcasters continue to make efficiency savings, it becomes more and more difficult to live within the income while delivering programme promises. High-quality programmes cost a lot in terms of attracting the talent, the resources needed to make them and the effort in research or news gathering. You cannot have high quality on the cheap. What you have to do is to cut the cloth to make it go further, maintaining quality standards while trying to cut costs.

Technology

This is an area fascinating to those inside broadcasting but often rather obscure to those outside of it. Let me single out a few key developments.

Digital compression. This means more channels in better quality. You can already watch Parliament from gavel to gavel on cable; the BBC now offers a Parliamentary service on its Digital Audio Broadcast (DAB) multiplex.

In September 1995, BBC Radio launched Europe's first DAB radio service, re-transmitting in CD-quality stereo the five national BBC networks. In July 1996, new services were piloted at the Radio Festival in Birmingham, demonstrating a range of experimental services including the instant information service called BBC Now. DAB will cover 60% of the population by 1997–98, though when it will become available commercially at a price we can all afford is a question only time and the radio manufacturers can answer. The BBC has kick-started DAB, and national commercial radio stations can extend their licence by eight years if they embrace this technology — a huge incentive. The race is now on for manufacturers to pick up the baton and run with it.

When the technology really takes off, the DAB radio receiver that we will all be putting on our birthday present list in 1998/99 will offer not just CD-quality radio sound and push-button tuning, but also options such as, perhaps, text with print-out facilities, alongside pictures or graphics. For radio lovers, Digital

Audio Broadcasting offers a truly exciting development — programmes are already being broadcast digitally, all we need are the radio receivers to enjoy them.

The digital revolution has begun. If DAB Radio is developing fast, digital satellite television has already started in France and the United States. BSkyB is committed to the creation of several hundred digital channels on satellite. Digital terrestrial television (DTT) has had its first demonstration to British broadcasters in 1996, and the 1996 Broadcasting Act allows for the introduction of DTT by the end of 1998. This brings the possibility of wide-screen flat TVs with additional complementary services available to viewers. So while we watch *Eastenders* or *Coronation Street*, we might want to find out more about a member of the cast or the story-line we missed the week before. DTT makes this possible. Whether or not Digital Terrestrial can compete with Digital Satellite remains to be seen.

Digital editing. The ability to 'cut' tape electronically in at your desk or at home on a PC is already possible. Stand-alone digital tape editing has been with us for several years. The saving in studio time is obvious: you can in effect carry a radio studio in your brief-case. But this is only a stepping-stone towards more news services, many of them interactive and available on demand.

As with all digital technologies, digital editing is becoming industry-wide within radio and more portable by the day. Your train seat or hotel room can become a studio. Reporters are already editing 'on the road' and then transmitting their completed reports back to base down ISDN digital telephone lines. When broadcast, the quality is perfect.

Convergence is the buzzword of the digital revolution. It means the coming-together of separate technologies — television, radio, computer and telephone — into new systems of delivering news, information and entertainment services. It is quite possible that within a few years these four may be available in a single machine. Personal computers already carry television pictures and enable the user to send faxes by modem. Crystal-ball gazing is an inexact science, so it is a matter of pure guesswork to predict how fast or what combinations the consumers of Britain will take up the new technologies. But the opportunities are endless.

Will cable overtake satellite? Will we want to trade in our televisions for high-tech versions? Will DAB radios replace our old transistors within the next five years? It's estimated that annually over half a million households invest in additional television services. By 2005, more than half of UK households are likely to be receiving multi-channel services by satellite, cable, terrestrial or telecom wires. All this suggests a future living room with a large flat-screen digital television receiver with high-definition pictures. The PC will have television facilities as a matter of course. And many will buy set-top boxes which enable viewers to add extra services to their televisions, though they will probably have to pay for those services. Convergence is with us, giving us more choice and a lot more confusion in its path.

The information superhighway — the Internet. This is a formidable new medium creating excitement and scepticism in equal quantity. Those with no experience of the Internet find it baffling. But the idea is very simple — a world of virtual reality in which computers talk to one another and enable computer users to talk to one another. It is not hard to use. My eleven-year daughter Bryony sometimes heads off to a local café in the London suburb where we live. It's part of the Cyberia chain. For under £2, on her very first visit, she was able to sit at a computer in the cafe and swap messages with other Internet users in such places as Canada, the United States, Hawaii and Zambia for half an hour. The technology is much easier to use than most people realise. Isabelle, her twin, is equally adept.

Many news organisations have a big presence on the Internet, from the BBC and Time-Warner to the *Daily Telegraph*, *The Times* and even *Playboy*. The Internet has massive implications, even more so for newspapers than for broadcast news-providers. Writing in the *Guardian* (*24* April 95) American commentator Jon Katz put it like this. 'Almost everything a newspaper used to do, somebody else is doing more quickly, more attractively, more efficiently and in a more interesting unfettered way.' For him, a key moment occurred in January 1994 when a PC with modem was used to flash news via the Internet of the Los Angeles earthquake before CNN or the Associated Press news agency could report it. Within minutes, subscribers had pinpointed the quake location, notified distant relatives and organised rescues. If the Internet continues to grow at its current speed (and over 25,000,000 people have access at the moment) its impact on our lives could be as significant as the invention of the printing press.

It is a resource available to all news providers. In August 1995,

Is More News Good News? 35

BBC Radio 4 ran a special Saturday night production called 'Reap the Whirlwind' to mark the fiftieth anniversary of Hiroshima. Listeners heard for the very first time voices of survivors from Hiroshima who had never spoken about their ordeal before. How did the BBC find them? They were located and contacted by means of the Internet. It is already proving its use as a production tool.

When I was a Foreign Duty Editor in the late 1980s, coming from a current affairs background, I was sent on overseas assignments to work with correspondents in the field. The G7 Summit in Venice in 1987 was one such occasion. With me were three BBC Correspondents and a reporter from *The Financial World Tonight*. One night we were working late on an item for the *Today* programme. The Italians had locked up the studios. So we had to return to our hotel and improvise. We took out the skirting board and wired a sound-enhancing device called a Mutterbox into the phone junction box to send our report back to London. It was like a good-quality telephone line but fell short of studio quality. It was broadcast. Nowadays, a telephone-quality feature would not be acceptable. Digital phone lines and satellite phones have improved quality beyond recognition.

Ten years later I was in Moscow to broadcast a live programme from Red Square as midnight struck on New Year's Eve 1991. I was there with presenter Robin Lustig to broadcast a live edition of *The World Tonight* to mark the end of the Soviet Union. We had all sorts of problems. Our radio mikes would not work in Red Square, so we had to put correspondent Bridget Kendall on a hotel balcony overlooking the square, holding a microphone on a long lead. This led into our hotel room which we had transformed into a radio studio with the help of some mattresses against the walls and a table we 'borrowed' from the hotel restaurant. We had a satellite dish perched on my fridge linked to an international maritime satellite as a back-up if our line went down. But as we went live on air, none of could have anticipated that the first two minutes of the broadcast (which won two awards) would be almost obliterated by the sound of loud explosions, as Moscow witnessed its biggest and loudest firework display. It was later alleged that CNN had paid for the fireworks display to brighten up their coverage!

So, ten years after Venice, we had abandoned the Mutterbox and telephone and switched to satellite technology and live co-presented programmes. By the time I went to South Africa in April 1994, the world had moved on again. There we had a strong BBC representation, with many programmes sending small production teams. Competition with our rivals was as strong as ever. Covering one story, a vicious attack was carried out on a black American journalist at a rally of far-right extremists. A commercial radio reporter beat everyone else on to air with the story, with the help of his state-of-the-art digital technology.

The BBC's coverage gained immeasurably from its technical facilities — computers linking the South African operation to production offices in London. I could write a script in South Africa and print it out seconds later in London. I was able to read the London-based presenter's cues into my interviews as he wrote them. I had three sound engineers at my disposal and a small fleet of radio cars. BBC reporters took digital phones with them and the means to make quality broadcasts from anywhere in South Africa. As a result, on the night Nelson Mandela declared his victory to his faithful ANC supporters in a Johannesburg hotel, listeners to Radio 5 Live heard the normal programmes interrupted by BBC correspondent Fergal Keane's voice demanding on air that the network join him. They then heard the triumphant cheering and ululations with the tongue that Africans so enjoy as Fergal described the event unfolding before his eyes. He described Nelson Mandela accepting the cheers, listeners heard him say live 'the hour has come' and then dance with delight. Within minutes everyone was singing that wonderful anthem 'God Bless Africa'. It made spellbinding radio — and it was live.

Another example came with the announcement of the IRA ceasefire. This was Radio 5 Live in the rough and raw, as Northern Ireland Correspondent Mark Devenport interrupted the *Magazine* programme to bring some momentous news. Mark was so anxious to break the news ahead of everyone else that he could barely find the breath to tell the world of the IRA ceasefire. His breathlessness and the edge of excitement in his voice was unforgettable to the listeners and helped to secure for the programme the Sony Award for Best Response to a News Event.

Technology is a driving force in radio. Bringing the news to listeners live and raw brings with it some editorial risks, but it also gives it an edge and excitement that audiences seem to want.

Audience demands

I think it fair to say that all news organisations, whether in print journalism or broadcast news, are more aware than ever before of what our audiences want from us. This can sway editorial values. But even when we are committed to impartial, fair and balanced coverage, it is still easy to come unstuck. ITN's reporter who followed Eric Cantona on his Caribbean holiday won little sympathy when the soccer player gave him short shrift. The publication of photographs of the Princess of Wales at the gym did nothing to enhance the reputation of the paper that printed them.

Broadcasters know a lot about our audiences and they are not slow to tell us what they think! But habits are changing too. Listeners are more promiscuous than ever, and are beginning to hop across radio channels far more than before. Audience research suggests that listeners and viewers want greater diversity, more specialism and immediacy. Although there will always be a fixed place for the regular news bulletin when people can catch up with the world, future audiences will want more information available when they want it at any time of the day or night. This won't just be new headlines and stories, but financial news, traffic information, weather updates and sports news too. Personal relevance will be a factor too — they will want documentaries and current affairs programming that that is targeted specifically to their interests and addresses their problems. That's why a twenty-four hour network is so useful.

In five or ten years' time we may even be able to devise our own news bulletin and select the stories we like in the order we want. Consumers, viewers and listeners will then manipulate virtually any kind of electronic information in almost any way we want.

Let me put my cards on the table now and speak personally. I welcome the proliferation of news services. I like the fact that listeners and viewers have more choice than ever before. Competition sharpens us, and can drive quality up as well as down. I must be honest and say that I welcome the changes taking place — but not uncritically. We have considered the driving forces. How might we respond?

I will begin with my personal response, as a journalist who is a Christian.

A CHRISTIAN PERSPECTIVE

Broadcast news worth having must embrace truth, and not as a relative value. For the Christian broadcaster, truth is an absolute value of infinite worth. Christians believe in a God who has revealed himself ultimately in a human life — through Jesus Christ. For the Christian believer, there is ultimate truth revealed in the person and work of Jesus Christ; in how he lived, why he died and in the convincing evidence for his resurrection. Truth's role in society is to set humankind free indeed. News stories can play a key part in revealing that ultimate truth about the nature of man and ultimately of man's relationship with God himself. Jesus himself knew how useful news events could be to illustrate a bigger truth.

Truth must be the cornerstone

I don't need to remind Christian how important truth is, nor that Jesus Christ claimed to be himself the way, the truth and the life (John 14). But Jesus also used parables to convey truth, and referred to news events of his day to illustrate his teaching. My favourite example of this is in Luke 13:1–9, where Jesus uses two news events as illustrations. Both, as it turns out, are disaster stories. Here is the passage with the news references in bold type:

> At that time there were some people present who told Jesus about **the Galileans whose blood Pilate had mixed with their sacrifices**. He answered them: 'Do you imagine that, because these Galileans suffered this fate, they must have been greater sinners than anyone else in Galilee? I tell you they were not; but unless you repent, you will all of you come to the same end. Or the **eighteen people who were killed when the tower fell on them at Siloam** — do you imagine they were more guilty than all the other people living in Jerusalem? I tell you they were not; but unless you repent, you will all of you come to the same end.'
>
> He told them this parable: 'A man had a fig-tree growing in his vineyard; and he came looking for fruit on it, but found none. So he said to the vine-dresser, "Look here! For the last three years I have come looking for fruit on this fig-tree without finding any. Cut it down. Why should it go on using up the soil?" But he replied, "Leave it, sir, this one year while I dig round it and manure it. And if it bears fruit next season, well and good; if not, you shall have it down."'

First there is the reference to the Galileans murdered by Pilate in the middle of their sacrifices. Pilate had decided that Jerusalem needed a new improved water supply. He planned to fund its construction using money taxed from the Jewish Temple. It was a good project but not surprisingly, there was uproar that the Romans were to use Jewish money to finance the work. Commentators believe that there was a public protest. Pilate instructed his soldiers to mingle with the mob, with cloaks over their battle dress, and to bring out their cudgels when the sign was given and disperse the crowd. But like so many civil riots in our own day, this one went wrong. The soldiers used violence in excess of their instructions and many people were killed.

The second news story is the death of eighteen people killed when the tower in Siloam collapsed on top of them. One commentator has suggested that the disaster was seen as retribution for local labourers accepting work on Pilate's hated aqueducts.

Jesus picked up on this feeling to say in no uncertain terms that the nation is a unit, chooses its own policy and must live with the consequences. The nation which rebels against God is on its way to disaster. How significant it is — and how useful to us as we consider tonight's subject — that Jesus then tells the parable of the fig-tree. I want to suggest that this can be read by us as the Parable of the News Provider.

The Parable of the News Provider

The fig tree (like the broadcaster) occupies a special place in some societies. In ancient Palestine, the fig tree could grow even in the poor and shallow soil found in vineyards. Trees were grown wherever there was soil. But soil was itself a precious commodity. If a fig tree bore no fruit it was cut down. What the grower wanted was a tree that bore fruit, that was productive and efficient with high-quality taste and lots of flavour. The broadcast news media should be like the fig tree. Are we being fruitful and productive? Are we giving back to society more than we are taking out of it? Are we providing good food for thought, texture to savour and adding flavour to our society — 'salt and light', if you like, to use the biblical metaphor? Or are we being parasites, using our favoured position to exploit others and to make money, flattering, perhaps, to deceive? How many of us will fall victim to our own hype? Do we live up to our promise? I would like to suggest that if we seek a theology of news, this is a good place to start.

Jesus the News-Maker

Jesus himself constantly made news. His death and resurrection are the most significant news events in the history of the world. Two thousand years later, the impact of those events continues to reverberate around the world. Sometimes what Jesus did was as much a commentary on his times and on the condition of humanity as what he said. Look at the dramatic event that followed Jesus entry into Jerusalem on Palm Sunday — his cleansing of the Temple. He overturned the tables of the money-changers. The relevance of this will be with us as long as there are those who will stop at nothing to generate wealth.

Every generation has its tales of financial disaster. Whether it be the South Sea Bubble or the Wall Street Crash, Black Wednesday or Barings Bank losing £900,000,000 on derivative trading in Singapore, the lesson is the same. Jesus' clearing-out of the money-changers from the house of God showed that God and Mammon can never easily co-exist. A clear distinction must be made between what is God's and what belongs to another world altogether.

Money is not wrong in itself. It is neutral. What counts is how we use it. Are we good stewards of what we have been given? It is the *love* of money which is the root of evil. Likewise, the broadcast news media are not intrinsically good or evil in themselves. They do belong in this world; but like every gift of God, they do have within them the potential to bring great benefit to the world in which live, and in which we are fellow-workers in partnership with God. Ultimately, the media exist like all created things for the glory of God, to show the world who God really is and to reveal ultimate truth. Like the fig tree, we have a responsibility as broadcasters to put in more than we extract. Ultimately, news should be honest and true and bring glory to God.

In his letter to the church at Philippi, the apostle Paul told his friends to grasp

> All that is true, all that is noble, all that is just and pure, all that is loveable and gracious, whatever is excellent and admirable — fill all your thoughts with these things. The lessons I taught you, the tradition I have passed on, all that you heard me say or saw me do, put into practice. (Philippians 4:8–9 NEB).

Sound advice, not just for first-century Christians but for twenty-first-century Christian broadcasters too.

Adding texture to society

Broadcast news should improve the texture of our lives. Quality news can help to replenish and reinvigorate us — it should challenge our assumptions, open our eyes and even inspire us into action. That it has that capability is not in question. The radio broadcasts of my colleague Mike Wooldridge and the television films of Michael Buerk opened all our eyes to the Ethiopian famine. Even rock stars were moved to use their massive appeal to raise money for the needy through Band Aid, though sadly the music industry has lacked the staying power of our comedy stars, who with Comic Relief are making a significant and impressive contribution.

Any gardener will tell you that the addition of organic material can make all the difference to a sticky soil. Organic matter helps to retain moisture and nutrients. So too, quality broadcast news can enrich our society. Let us encourage a news culture that has this role. All of us need news that helps us to understand our world and makes sense of it. News should add to our lives, not take away from it.

Even reporting something like the House of Commons can be done in such a way as to show the full range of political opinion and what unites as well as divides our political leaders. A striking example of this was the speeches given after the tragic death of the then Labour Party leader John Smith. What John Major and Margaret Beckett had to say then, their voices full of emotion, shattered the stereotype of Parliamentary broadcasting.

The bigger agenda must include faith

From a Christian viewpoint, I would also want to argue passionately for a wider news agenda that covers all the affairs of humanity and not just the political and economic spheres of British society.

Coverage of social affairs, health issues and education has improved in recent years. The increase in the number of specialist correspondents within the BBC has helped considerably. At a time when many national newspapers are cutting back overseas posts, it is good to see the likes of the BBC and ITN committed to covering the difficult foreign stories like Rwanda, Somalia and Bosnia. But I must also confess to a sense of disappointment that the coverage of the spiritual life of Britain across the media of religious affairs is arguably repetitious rather inadequate in comparison with our coverage of health or education or even football. It is not enough to judge how much interest there is in moral and spiritual issues by the numbers who go to church each Sunday; but even they often outnumber those who attend football matches on a Saturday afternoon.

I want to argue for a broader news agenda that recognises that there is spiritual life in Britain and a vibrant and in many areas growing religious community. The churches have a voice and need to be heard. So does the Muslim community. I think you can even argue a case for designer Buddhists. Our news should reflect the whole of Britain back to Britain. No section of our society, young or old, secular or Christian, should be marginalised.

A broader news agenda and wider choice is only worth having if the sum total of it is adding something of quality. But many broadcasting innovations are like novelty breakfast cereals — a new taste that does not sustain one's interest for long. The old faithful hang on to live another day. Look at how well the radio phone-in has survived and prospered. On the late lamented LBC, George Gale and Brian Hayes turned the phone-in from virtual cost-free radio into something worth hearing. They were pioneers. On LBC's religious weekend programming, John Forrest used the format for a topical religious discussion called 'We Believe', which I had the pleasure of developing and presenting with him. The topical phone-in with guests gave the format an edge and immediacy. Despite early misgivings by many media commentators, the phone-in format has added a dimension to our broadcasting. At its best, it makes for riveting radio. At its worst, it provides entertainment of rare and dubious value. The style of broadcasting it helped to spawn has itself grown into something new. Talk Radio UK offers an alternative and accessible national speech network to the richer and more intelligent mix of BBC Radio 4.

I believe that the bigger agenda must embrace life in all its fullness, which will include spiritual life as well. That's what I call real added value! Life is more than a series of events. Life is not just the sum of events in a news diary or what happens between the Queen's speech and the next Parliamentary recess. It is more than the FTSE Index, the latest traffic foul-up on the M25 and the shipping forecast. Our news values should reflect humanity itself in all its God-given glory, with more about people and their lives and less about political process and events. Let's have more people-driven news in a broad context, and less of the news agenda dictated from Westminster or Wall Street.

RISKS AND DANGERS

We have more choice — but at what price? What are the risks and dangers that the growth in news has brought?

Truth become a casualty of speed

As broadcasters become more competitive, the temptation to get on the air as fast as possible will increase. Radio 5 Live's brief is to be first and live. Its editors take great and justifiable pride in broadcasting a breaking story. When Mark Devenport told the nation the IRA had announced a ceasefire, he was still short of breath in his rush to the studio. It won the Magazine programme a Sony Award.

I have also seen a newsreader go into a studio to read out a news summary on the hour only to find a major news story breaking on the agency wires within a minute of going on air (a far more common occurrence than you might think). An electricity board announced the closure of dozens of retail outlets, with the loss of thousands of jobs. The news reader read it directly, on air, off the computer screen in the studio. Now, the story came from an authoritative, reliable source and there was no reason to doubt it. So no check phone-calls were made to confirm the details. But what if it had turned out to be wrong? As soon as you broadcast news that is not accurate, your credibility and authority disappears. No journalist can take a risk not getting it right. Accuracy is everything.

It is so easy for the modern high-tech radio station to try to be quick off the mark and to get it wrong. We all make mistakes. I once worked on a news programme in which a reporter did a piece on the decline of British film comedy. How sad it was, he said, that so many 'Carry On' stars had died, such as Sid James and Charles Hawtrey. Two hours later, Charles Hawtrey rang up to tell us he was alive and well! He could have taken legal action, but instead he was happy for us to broadcast an apology the following morning.

Some of the signals reaching us from the United States are worrying. American talk radio is de-regulated radio at its worst;

automobile-friendly with larger-than-life radio stars who attract millions of listeners. The most successful of the so-called 'shock jocks' take a hard right-wing view. Convicted Watergate criminal G. Gordon Liddy is one of their stars. Another, Rush Limbaugh, attracts 25,000,000 listeners. He has a huge presence on the Internet too. Some polls have suggested that 44% of Americans named talk radio as their chief source of political information. The worry is that their political views are presented as not just opinion, but information.

The audience believe what they hear even though many of these performers seem to have little regard for truth or accuracy. The danger is that American shock jocks can easily be manipulated by pressure groups. According to one report, they appear free to broadcast anything, however libellous, inflammatory or untrue, without any control or check.

There is a hideous expression used by American journalists. 'If it bleeds — it leads.' The famous O. J. Simpson car chase, carried live across the US television networks, has fuelled the fire. Many stations now run what they call action news. Within the first minute comes guaranteed live action. It may be a helicopter watching a car chase. it may be a police siege or shoot-out. Viewers know that anything can happen — an arrest, a chase or even watching someone killed or murdered live on television. With live all-action television news, editorial control goes out of the window. The event determines the news. There are no safety nets.

That is one American product that I have no desire to see here in the UK. We have been spared so far — but the seeds are being sown. We are beginning to see live action documentaries using video clips taken by police cars and helicopters chasing speeding vehicles or escaping criminals. The emergency services use video extensively and are making more of this material available to broadcasters to repackage. The first British live two-hour documentary special to watch police patrols late on a Friday night turned out, in my opinion, to be stupefyingly dull, unless watching drunken revellers in Newcastle City Centre is your kind of entertainment. But the American live-action genre remains a threat to our screens and to our intelligence.

In Britain, guidelines on violence are getting tighter, so here the trend is going the other way. What was acceptable even two years ago would not be acceptable now. Taste and decency issues, strong language and unjustified violence provoke strong audience reaction that has encouraged the broadcasters to tighten up their self-regulation. The BBC's Programme Complaints Unit and the Independent Television Commission both play key roles in this process. The amalgamation of the Broadcasting Standards Council and Complaints Commission into a single body will also ensure that broadcasters do not back-peddle on these issues.

I suspect that the greater danger is not that of over-dramatising the news but of sanitising it. The massacres in Rwanda are a holocaust, but such is the horror and scale of the killing that it has not been easy to convey its full extent. Fergal Keane did a chilling television report on the massacres, but one wonders how many viewers turned off or switched over, unable to take in the sight of wall-to-wall bodies in one compound he entered. George Alagiah has also done some remarkable work in this area, worthy of the finest traditions of journalism.

In radio, the concern over taste and decency is shared. There was much concern when Talk Radio was launched promising frankness and the first UK 'shock jocks'. But the launch backfired badly on the station and the policy (and management) was rapidly abandoned. Now it is settling down under new management and ownership to offer a version of talk radio that we can recognise and enjoy without fear of American-spun excesses creeping in. Libel laws are very tough in Britain, but privacy laws are not. Self-regulation is constantly at risk from the efforts of some tabloid newspapers chasing some latest sex scandal. There are always dangers. However, I am reasonably confident that the excesses of the American brand will stay firmly on the other side of the Big Pond.

Creeping trivialisation

The competition for audiences could have another serious side-effect.

There is a real and potent danger that we could see a decline in standards of journalism. We have suggested that truth may become a casualty of speed. But news values themselves in broadcasting could follow the well-trodden Fleet Street path if we are not careful. I would hate to see the national tabloid pap broadcast news agenda — but it could happen.

There are concerns in our industry that the excesses of the tabloids might begin to drive the agenda for quality newspapers and for broadcasters too. We must not lose the range and breadth and depth of stories and issues that we cover now. The word 'significance' has become a key word in defining BBC news values. It means that we run stories because they matter. Just because a story has appeared elsewhere does not mean other news outlets have to mimic their rivals and follow suit. Let's aim to stick to what is important, what affects people's lives, what really matters.

Loss of quality and minority programming

Meeting the demands of an ever diversified audience should broaden our programming. But if the need to build big audiences and attract heavy advertising takes over, then this will put at risk the kind of programme that is never going to have mass appeal. When the ITV franchises were re-allocated, some fine weekly current affairs programmes like *This Week* and *First Tuesday* were dropped. *World In Action* survived and carried the flag for independent television current affairs. In the BBC, there has been much innovation. *Here and Now* is a welcome addition — a populist current affairs programme of wide audience appeal. *Correspondent* does for television what *From our own Correspondent* has long done for radio. There is scope for more specialist news programmes. But broadcasters must guard against commercial pressures reducing the range.

DEATH BY RATINGS

That is why ratings must never be the sole arbiter of taste. It would be tragic if ratings became the measure by which the quality of programmes was measured. Journalistic standards of accuracy, impartiality, fairness, and a commitment to truth should be our guiding lights, not ratings.

News at Ten has survived various pressures to move its slot so that ITV can show full-length feature films uninterrupted by news bulletins. But will it be able to do so in the longer term, as the battle for ratings increases?

If we find ourselves importing the *Action News* values I described earlier, then ratings will grow in importance. News can be popular without becoming tabloid. One American television station has the philosophy of 'people-izing' stories. In other words, you don't start with an issue, with the facts or with the news event, as we might here. You always start with an individual and build out from that. So every news story has a personal human dimension to it, good or bad. There is nothing wrong with this *per se*, but it does narrow your view and can distort it. You can talk about the fishing dispute between Canada and Spain by showing how one Canadian fisherman's livelihood is threatened by big Spanish trawlers. But are you telling the whole story? Are you also going to visit Spain and see the impact on the Spanish lives affected?

The real danger of the 'ratings-first' approach is that it breaks down the distinction between the lives of ordinary people and those in the public eye. Reporting that some politician has a secret lover, or following every twist and turn in a royal marriage-separation-divorce saga, may be terrific for the tabloid press but is not always appropriate for television news. When ITN followed Eric Cantona on holiday after his 'kung fu' incident, was it an invasion of his privacy or was he fair game in the public interest? 'Public interest' can be one justification too far at times.

Information apartheid

The new digital revolution will change all of our lives. For those who are equipped with it, the new technology offers the possibility of instant access to more information than we can handle — including news on tap. One group of journalists will be able to produce news for a variety of outlets. But what of those who do not have access? What if the information super highway is a no through road? How will Africa fare in the digital new world order? A Channel 4 series called *Visions of Heaven and Hell* looked at both sides of the argument. The series found plenty of advocates who see the new technology bringing new and greater freedom and excitement to our lives; virtual reality will become an alternative reality. But the series also spoke to those who argue that technology is already pulling us apart. The world will divide, some believe, into the technologically rich and the technologically poor, living side-by-side in loathing and fear. They used the phrase 'global apartheid'.

For me, one statistic from the series hit me like a hammer. In Africa there are some 500,000 million people. In the city of Tokyo there are only 8 million people. Yet they have in that one city three times more telephone lines than in the whole of Africa. And now there are plans to invest more and more in telecommunications in Tokyo, and not a single penny in Africa. Why bother to invest in Africa? There's no money there.

Technology does not recognise frontiers, so it has the ability to unite us and to fragment us. It doesn't care who gets left behind. Those who are not computer-literate may find their lack of skills will widen the gap between the haves and have-nots. If news becomes a big user of the superhighway, there will be those in the know and those denied this information. In that, real dangers lie.

THE OPPORTUNITIES MORE NEWS BRINGS

News can liberate

Information is important. It can liberate and free our thinking and equip us to make decisions and make sense of the world in which we live. How much longer would it have taken the inhabitants of the German Democratic Republic to see through the lies, the follies and structural weaknesses of Eastern bloc communism, had it not been for the invasion of their thinking by international radio or the availability of West German television? It wasn't watching J. R. Ewing in *Dallas* that fired them up. Hearing and seeing their world through different eyes was just one of the catalysts for change.

Radio and television played a crucial role in the events of 1989 in Germany which ended Communism and brought reunification. News can liberate just by changing our perceptions, by making us aware that change is possible, that renewal of people and nations can happen. The words of Jesus, that the truth will set us free and make us free indeed, have stood the test of time.

News transcends nations

Information does not respect boundaries or nationalities. It crosses frontiers without respect or regard for political, or for that matter religious, ideology. Faced with alternative versions of reality, people begin to make decisions. This can empower them. The result may not always be one we would welcome. One of the saddest spectacles since the Berlin Wall came down in November 1989 has been the disillusionment and distress of high-minded East Germans, with a view of statehood that embraced social welfare and thought unemployment intolerable. In the West they found the means to create and increase wealth, but they also found that capitalism has winners and losers and rich and poor.

As I have indicated, those of us who are purveyors of news need the most rigorous standards to make sure we get it right. Sloppy journalism can lead to a distorted view of the world. Crime is an example.

Getting it right: Crime

Crime is a major public concern, and our audiences get much of their information about it from us. It is so easy to mislead. For example: few crimes horrify us more than an older person being mugged or murdered. The sight of someone in their seventies with swollen lips, black eyes and bruising turns our stomachs. We are rightly filled with revulsion at such pictures. Because these pictures are so graphic and powerful, newspapers and television are very likely to show them at every opportunity. The impact can be colossal, with older people frightened of leaving their homes, or even of opening their front door. We, the audience, gain the impression that violent crime is one of society's biggest problems.

It is true that crime recorded by the police has doubled over the past decade, and that most crimes are never reported to the police. But it is also true that violent crime is a small proportion of all recorded crime: just 5%. Rape, too, is a tiny proportion: 1% of that 5%. Britain sits low down the European league-table of violent crime. But for vehicle crime, we come top. The reality is that 95% of recorded crime in the UK is not against people but against property. Apart from big robberies, most of this goes unreported in the broadcast media.

And what impression do we get of criminals? Do we have a visual image of middle-aged hardened criminals in balaclavas? Do we think of the late Buster Edwards or Ronnie Kray as the archetypal villain? If we do, we are wrong. Criminals are overwhelmingly male and young. One-third of all men have been found guilty of an indictable offence by the age of thirty.

So the lessons for the broadcast journalism committed to truth and fair coverage are that we should recognise the danger of adding to our audience's fear of becoming victims. Statistically, they are very unlikely to do so. Our coverage needs to put the crime we are reporting into a wider context. Because news reflects the unusual it is always at risk of presenting a distorted view of reality. To redress this, in the BBC we now have guidelines for journalists reporting crime and monitoring procedures to ensure we avoid some of these traps. These include suggesting a trend where none exists (just because one attack comes two days after another does not mean that there is a link between the crimes), and use of unnecessarily graphic details, particularly when children may be listening or viewing.

Quality counts

Given more news available on demand at the push of a button or on the end of an icon on our omni-present PC or TV, what is to distinguish one news provider from another? The answer must be 'quality'. What we will choose to watch and hear will be the news service that we can trust — that provides us with the information we want in the format we like. It must be distinctive, and must carry with it the conviction and authority we expect from our news providers. But because it is reaching us so quickly now, news is becoming less processed than ever before. We are seeing it in its most raw state. News conferences are being broadcast live with instant commentary. This in itself brings the risk of news that is not digested and is therefore indigestible.

There is a danger that context will be forgotten and the big picture get lost in the rush for the immediate, the available and sometimes the trivial. Here we must learn a lesson from our colleagues in the United States. Obsession with crime, with legal coverage, with sifting evidence and speculating on events before they take place is a road that can lead to nowhere.

Making sense of the world

Providing a context and a deeper and wider understanding of news events is important. This is one of the great strengths of programmes like *The World Tonight* or *Newsnight*. There is a great opportunity for newsmakers to help each of us understand the world in which we live — God's world. Part of our mission must be to make sense of the world.

In reporting the truth, journalists are continuing the process that Jesus endorsed: to set people free by telling them the truth. For the Christian journalist, this has a special meaning, for to us it is the truth about Jesus himself — who he is, why he died, how he rose — that changes our world view and sets us on to a new road of freedom. This road starts at the Cross and ends in repentance and faith and life eternal. In reporting the truth, the world as it really is, we are part of that democratic process that sets people free. This is God's democracy.

Providing background and context is not always easy. There is sometimes a fine line between simple, concise and uncomplicated explanation, and the kind of overcomplicated elaboration of which some correspondents are guilty. Many journalists were themselves confused in the 1995 conflict between Canada and Spain over fish. It took several days for it to become clear that what we call turbot, the Canadians call Greenland or Newfoundland halibut. For a day or two, many journalists thought two fish were in dispute, not one! Context is only useful if it is easy to understand. How you package that can make a huge difference. Maps, graphs and bar charts can make it harder, not easier, to understand an economic story.

I want to end with a simple plea. If we are committed, as I am, to using the news media to make sense of the world, then we need those working within the media who see the bigger picture: in other words, who recognise God's role in all of this. My view (which, I said at the beginning, is a personal rather than a corporate view) is that I would love to see more Christians getting involved and working in the news media. I would love to see more discernment and judgement in what we cover, testing what is significant now — in worldly terms, certainly, but in spiritual terms as well.

Charles Dickens begins *A Tale of Two Cities*, his great novel on the French revolution, with these words. 'It was the best of times, it was the worst of times.' To many people, faced by the proliferation of broadcast news, there is the fear of news overload. These are 'the worst of times'. But we know too that in the increasingly competitive broadcasting environment, no organisation, whether much loved and respected or brand new and in search of a reputation, can sit back and be complacent. We turn to face the future with a sense of excitement and aware of all the opportunities ahead. These can also become 'the best of times'.

Is more news good news? I think it can be. The opportunity is there, alongside the pitfalls and the risks. Like the fig tree in Jesus' parable, the broadcast media have the capability of making a net positive contribution to our world that each of us can value. My hope is that more news will, indeed, be good news.

3: Never Mind the Quality, Feel the Ratings!

Graham Mytton

When I was asked to speak at this year's London Lectures my first reaction was to ask, why me? I have worked most of my adult life in the BBC, in both programme production and management, but I now hold what might be seen as a rather obscure job. I am responsible for all the BBC's audience research outside the UK, and also for the department that deals with the hundreds of thousands of letters received every year from all over the world. I am not at the centre of things, and am a long way away from those parts of Britain's television and radio which play such a major role in life in our country today.

Then I remembered Malcolm Muggeridge's book *Christ and the Media*, and remembered that it was the text of his own 1976 London Lectures. Those lectures (I didn't attend them, I read the book) had a major impact on me. They both inspired and infuriated, sometimes both at the same time, even in the same sentence. The book is still worth reading and should be reprinted. It is still, as the *Church of England Newspaper* commented at the time, 'marvellous, rumbustious argument, savagely satirical but shot through with a love of humanity.... wonderful reading'.

Malcolm began his first lecture, which was chaired by the then Director General of the BBC Sir Charles Curran, with these words.

> It is a truism to say that the media in general, and television in particular, and BBC television especially, are incomparably the greatest single influence in our society today, exerted at all social, economic and cultural levels. This influence, I should add, is, in my opinion, largely exerted irresponsibly, arbitrarily, and without reference to any moral or intellectual, still less spiritual guidelines whatsoever.[1]

---
[1] Malcom Muggeridge, *Christ and the Media* (Hodder and Stoughton, 1977), p23.

He had an almost entirely pessimistic view of the modern electronic media in which he had spent so much of his professional life. Like many others, I felt then and since that what he said, although characteristically and outrageously exaggerated, contained much that was true. Muggeridge pointed to the false values of so much that is portrayed and of the temptations put before us in the media by the nature of what we are doing. He challenged Christians to think about the special features of radio and television, especially their power to inform and influence the minds of millions of people, power which is often used in a trivialising and distorting way. And I believe as a Christian that the way we use our mass media, either as producers or consumers, is a profoundly moral issue that lifts it above the commonplace.

That is in fact what Muggeridge often did in his use of television and radio. He lifted things above the ordinary, despite the fact that he had an rather baleful view of his own contribution, probably from a fear of the temptations of vanity and pride that beset all of us who work in the media. He told of his horror when one day, having dozed in his sitting room, he woke up to the sound of his own voice and the sight of his own face on television. He decided there and then to 'have his aerials removed'.

But the fact that so much television is tawdry or of little consequence or value should not lead one to condemn the medium. You might as well condemn all magazines and journals because of what can be found on the newsagents' shelves, or refuse to go on using money because there is so much counterfeit money in circulation. For myself I am happy to go on owning television and radio if, from, time to time, they provide me with things that are memorable, worthwhile and of value. It is these aspects of broadcasting that I am addressing today. I want to stimulate thought and debate about the way we measure and assess the value of the broadcasting services we receive.

Although I was once a radio programme producer, my credentials for speaking on this subject at all are my twelve years in audience research for the BBC World Service. This experience has given me a particular, though I hope a relevant, perspective on broadcasting.[2]

Audience research has flourished in the management culture of the 1990s. You might expect me to be pleased at this state of affairs,

---

[2] The contents of this chapter, of course, reflect that perspective, and are personal opinion rather than BBC policy.

and on the whole I am. But it doesn't stop me questioning (as I shall be doing in this chapter) what I believe to be some of the false values that have been promoted by that management culture, and which are in danger of distorting the relationships between audience research and the people who make programmes. It is also distorting the ways in which audience research is being used. This is no obscure or *recherché* idea but is, as I hope to demonstrate, at the heart of the issues about public service broadcasting today. You have only to read the press, both broadsheet and tabloid, to see how often programmes and networks are judged not so much on their content or quality as on their ratings. To make a bad programme may be something to avoid; to make one that doesn't attract the millions is seen as the graver fault. Ratings do matter, of course, but they are surely not a primary way of judging the success or failure of all broadcasting ventures.

I want to look at what I believe to be the distortions of audience research brought about by the management culture of the 1990s. The trend over the past five years or so has been towards the greater use of performance indicators. If you are required to have performance indicators, then you have to find something to measure; and audience research is an obvious and convenient provider of the necessary figures. So there has been a massive increase in demand for measurements and figures of all kinds. It has been a period of great prosperity for audience research. The new-style managers are insatiably hungry for the data we produce.

In his James Cameron memorial lecture last year, John Tusa drew attention to this feature of the managerial revolution. He did so from the perspective of a creative broadcaster and programme maker, but also from that of someone who is no mean manager either, as he showed in his six distinguished years at the helm in Bush House. He was enormously supportive of audience research and greatly increased the resources put into it. He is in a better position than anyone else I know to say the following:

> Ultimately the management revolution runs into difficulties as soon as it becomes inappropriate to the activity it is trying to manage. Bent as it is on quantification, based as it is on measurement ... how does it deal with the unquantifiable, with quality, with inspiration? ... In a management culture where only numbers count, the uncountable is not only illegitimate, it is insignificant also.[3]

---

[3] John Tusa, 'Programmes or Products: The Management Ethos and Creative Values', James Cameron Memorial Lecture, City University, 14 June 1994.

We spend a lot of money on quantifying audiences and attempting to measure audience perceptions of programme quality. But there is a limit to what can be done, and I agree with John Tusa that too much is being asked of audience research. Many intelligent and creative broadcasters know its value and usefulness, but they also know its limits. The management culture of today has given it an exaggerated and distorted importance, and that has affected the way we audience researchers are being used.

In the days before this managerial revolution, our figures were often merely glanced at, perhaps with bored indifference, by producers who just knew that what they were doing reached a significant audience. They preferred to rely more on anecdotes and listeners' letters than on the more reliable methods of audience research — more reliable, that is, in proving something about the size and nature of that audience. But for some of my colleagues, the definition of good research was that which provided evidence to support their established beliefs. The BBC, certainly the World Service, had a self-confidence (some might call it arrogance) that it knew best. This attitude, once upon a time, was not unusual in domestic broadcasting either. When audience research was first under consideration in the BBC, just eight years after its foundation, Charles Siepmann the Director of Talks wrote:

> However complete and effective any survey we launch might be, I should still be convinced that our policy and programme building should be based first and last upon our conviction as to what should and should not be broadcast.[4]

This view, with which I agree to an extent, lived on in this undiluted form in Bush House until quite recently. But now it has changed completely and, I would argue, there is a danger that we may have now gone to the opposite extreme.

Measuring performance makes sense. But it becomes pathological when the measure comes to matter more than what you are measuring. We see the phenomenon in the United States, in a media environment that is largely ratings-driven; where fortunes, careers and reputations are destroyed or boosted absurdly by a few decimal points in audience share. Are we going in the same direction? Perhaps the difference here is that the change in the ratings has to be before,

---

[4] Quoted in Peter Menneer, '*Broadcasting Research*: Necessity or Nicety?' Intermedia, May 1984, Vol. 12, No. 3.

and not after, the decimal point! We have not yet gone the way of some public broadcasters in Europe who, desperate to retain audience share by any means possible, have outdone the commercial competition in the production of cheap and tawdry programming with high ratings. RAI, the public broadcaster in Italy, now produces very few documentary programmes. Its programmes for children are said by critics to contain little of real value or purpose beyond entertainment. RAI has been extraordinarily successful in retaining something approaching a 50% share of viewing, and this is often pointed to as a great achievement in a country with as much television competition Italy; but it has been at the cost of the loss of much that is worthwhile.

It might sound as if I am biting the hand that feeds me, or at least that I am being two-faced, for I have spent much of the past twelve years extolling the importance, even the essential qualities, of audience research.[5] I am not going to complain about the way my colleagues and superiors in the BBC World Service have responded to my blandishments over the past few years. Audience research at Bush House is certainly much better funded than it used to be. I calculate that we have received an 800% increase in real terms in the funds we have to spend on projects since I started in 1982. Audience research has become more professional, and IBAR, as the Research Department is known, has a world-wide reputation for both the quality and quantity of its work. It has pioneered research in many places and developed new uses of research.[6]

---

[5] You may be thinking that twelve years is rather a long time. It's said that one long-serving BBC employee was described by one of the many newcomers at the top of the Corporation as 'tainted by experience'! That seems to be either an affliction or a quality in audience research. In the 59 years since domestic audience research was begun by Robert Silvey in 1936, there have been only four Heads of Audience Research. Similarly, in the BBC World Service I am only the fourth person in charge since the Research Unit was formed nearly 50 years ago. Is it because we cling on to a wonderful job, or because everyone else says, behind our backs, 'leave well alone'? Is there some unwritten rule that you keep this job until you retire, die or are sacked? It's sobering to reflect that there have been more Popes and Archbishops of Canterbury in my lifetime than Heads of Audience Research at Bush House!

[6] For published examples of audience research for the World Service, see Graham Mytton (ed.) *Global Audiences: Research for Worldwide Broadcasting*, London: John Libbey, 1993; and Allen Cooper, Graham Mytton and Peter Stratton 'Effective Quality: A Performance Indicator for International Broadcasting', *Worldwide Electronic and Broadcast Audience Research Symposium*, the Advertising Research Foundation and the European Society for Opinion and Marketing Research. Paris, May 1994. Amsterdam: ESOMAR, 1994, Volume 2, pp. 79–96.

Nor am I going to question, or cast doubt on, the continuing importance and relevance of audience research. It is only through audience research that broadcasters are able to obtain reliable and comprehensive information about who is listening or viewing, or about how many there are at any time in the audience for any programme or service. In Britain, and in most developed countries, research is extensive and continuous so that my counterparts in Britain and elsewhere can calculate shares of listening or viewing between the networks, the reach of each network over a day or a week, and plot changes as the media landscape changes.

We can report detailed information about the audience — their age, geographical location, social class and much more besides. Audience research can provide data on appreciation and enjoyment. It can even occasionally tell us something about the way programmes and services are used, what people learn from what they see and hear and in what ways (if any) their behaviour or attitudes are changed as a result. Research can explore and test new programme formats. It is often used to find ways to improve the appeal of programmes; these techniques are most developed in the field of advertising. But the biggest part of our activity is in providing measurements. These are essential if any broadcasting manager is going to make the best use of resources. There are many other important uses of quantitative research. One is very important for a public service broadcaster. It is to show if certain sections of the public are being poorly served, in that their use of BBC TV or radio is well below the norm.

Broadcasting is a different kind of activity from most other services to the public. Unlike hospital managers we cannot count patients treated, or measure waiting times. Unlike rail chiefs, broadcasters cannot count tickets, although like them we can and do record delays, breakdowns and technical failures. Unlike the press, we cannot count sales. Radio and television stations, in their free-to-air format at least, have no sales figures. Obviously, we have to measure audiences by some other means.

Broadcasting needs research in ways that other forms of communication do not. I am speaking here today before an audience and can see how many of you have come to listen. I can see how many were attracted by the subject matter of my lecture, or of these lectures as a whole. I cannot easily tell what you think of what I am saying, how interesting you find it, whether I can be understood, or what you make of what I am saying. People are usually polite on these occasions; if I am being a bore, no one will tell me — but it will probably show sooner or later on your faces. With broadcasting, we have no such immediate feedback. If our output is going to be any good; if it is going to be capable of responding to audience demand and need; above all perhaps; if it is going to be publicly accountable, then audience research is an essential part of the process.

It is not always so in broadcasting. Many radio and television stations in today's world, perhaps the majority, get by with little or no audience research. This is so in most totalitarian and authoritarian states, especially those where state monopoly in broadcasting still prevails. When you listen to or watch much of their programme output, the absence of concern about what is happening at the receiving end is plain enough to see. When alternative services are available, especially those which pay attention to audience preferences and interests, the audiences migrate. That is why the BBC World Service's largest audiences are in such countries, where the state controls broadcasting or where poverty and underdevelopment restrict the choices available in the media. We often know more about audience behaviour, tastes and interests than the domestic state controlled stations do, a fact commented on recently in a Ukrainian newspaper which noted that we were carrying out some qualitative research there for the BBC's Ukrainian language service.

> It is surprising that our mass media don't care too much about their audience. But in the West, they treat this matter very seriously indeed. Experts from the BBC spent several days in Lviv. They did research into their audience, but the main thing was to find out about who might become listeners to the BBC World Service..... Meanwhile we are using the system of trial and error, relying to a great extent on our intuition. We should thank God when it doesn't let us down. But maybe a scientific approach would help too.[7]

Knowing the audience is an essential prerequisite to effective communication. When Paul preached in Athens he had obviously taken the trouble beforehand to find out something about the Athenians. Christ spoke in a different manner according not only to what he was saying, but also to whom he was saying it. The difference with broadcasting is that we have to rely on doing at least some research if we are going to find out.

[7] *Vsenukrainskiye Vedomosti*, Lviv, February 1995. Lviv, formerly Lvov, is a major regional capital of the Ukraine.

A commitment to seeking audience opinion and response in a systematic way was not always there in the BBC, either here in Britain or for our external services. For the first fourteen years of the BBC's existence, and for much longer in much other public broadcasting in Europe, there was no audience measurement, still less other kinds of research. But in 1936, Robert Silvey began to provide answers to the question that became the title of his book *Who's Listening?*[8] Since he began regular audience measurement and other research, the BBC has become accustomed to fairly comprehensive information about its audience in Britain.

There is surely no argument any longer about the essential nature of audience research. But other questions than 'Who's Listening?' are also important. Why do we want to know, and for what are we going to use the information? And are these measures to be used to evaluate our success or failure? And are they really what we want them to be?

Let us take the BBC World Service, now in its sixty-third year of service to the world. It is one of the most highly valued institutions in Britain, or so it is said. How can we say that? A Parliamentary Early Day Motion of support for the service attracted 408 MP's signatures, the third highest in Parliament's history. There were many favourable mentions at the recent Britain in the World Conference. There are the testimonies of thousands of British people abroad and of the thousands of travellers who tell us when they get home how valuable they find the service. What Terry Waite and Thomas Sutherland said about the World Service after their long incarceration in Lebanon were, for us who work in Bush House, very gratifying expressions of what we see as one of the main purposes of all our activity. Letters from people who live under repressive regimes can be powerful evidence also. Here is what two Burmese listeners recently wrote:-

> The BBC has transformed into our organ. We have accorded it this status, not the UK government.

> The BBC is the most important thing in our lives. If we [can't hear it] it's like living in darkness.

But these are typical letters from committed and dedicated listeners in a totalitarian state. What of people who don't take up pen to write

---
[8] Robert Silvey, *Who's Listening?: The Story of BBC Audience Research* (George Allen and Unwin, 1974).

and who don't live in such difficult circumstances? After carrying out some extensive research recently in seventeen different countries, the British research agency MBL had this to say about what listeners think of the World Service:

> The BBC World Service has the following values:
> It is beyond national politics and commercial interests
> But has characteristics that are typically British
> It sends out and receives information from around the world
> It knows and respects local culture
> It is uniquely concerned with the truth
> It does things as they should be done
> It plays a parental, authoritative role. It reflects timeless values
> It is respected and loved

The agency provided many quotes to back up this view. The following is typical. It is a response to a question that formed part of the MBL research: 'If the BBC died, what would its obituary say?'

> Here lies someone from far away, who came to revolutionise the history of Brazilian communication. From that moment on, the level of journalism changed, benefiting from your [the BBC's] experience, and your standards, it was to be a different vision of the news and how it should be presented, those who made use of your standards and knowledge definitely benefited.

This research provided valid evidence that we have something here of considerable value and importance. It gives support to the words of the World Service's statement of purpose, published in its Annual Report in 1991.

> Free and untainted information is a basic human right. Not everyone has it; almost everyone wants it. It cannot by itself create a just world, but a just world order can never exist without it.
>
> The BBC World Service aims to be trusted by its audience, independent of political partisanship and commercial pressures. It reflects the world to the world, promotes a common understanding and shared experience between people of different nationalities and cultures.[9]

That is an excellent summary of how we see our role. It is an inspiring statement which also rings true. We find in much of our qualitative research that there is a remarkable degree of harmony between what the BBC aims to achieve, as outlined here, and the perception people have of what it actually does. They do mostly find the BBC trustworthy. They do value its integrity and freedom.

---
[9] BBC World Service Annual Plan, 1991–92, p.3.

Listeners are often critical too, especially if they discern what they perceive as political bias. We seek to understand listener opinion and provide answers to criticism. Obviously, it also matters very much to find out just who and how many are listening. According to evidence from our surveys, in 100 countries, over 130,000,000 people listen to the BBC World Service radio on a weekly basis. We have not yet been able to obtain data from every country, so that figure does not include listeners in China, Burma, Iran, Iraq, Libya, Cuba, Afghanistan and a few others. But this figure (our latest estimate is 133,000,000) is in danger of being given an importance far greater than anything else. It is absurd to elevate the numbers of people listening to be the sole, or even the most important, measure of value.

What determines whether something is worthwhile? If this lecture venue of St Peters is packed today, does that mean that my lecture is any better than if it were empty? One useful indicator might be if you all stayed to the end! But that might be more a measure of your good manners than of the quality of my lecture. For me, and I hope for the Institute of Contemporary Christianity, the main measure of the success of this lecture will be whether it makes any impact on anyone; if you go away having enjoyed a pleasant and stimulating evening; if what I say stimulates debate and discussion about the way we assess the value and importance of different broadcasts and services. I don't necessarily want everyone to agree with what I am saying, but I do want people who hear me, or read what I say later, to challenge the fashionable assumptions that are so often made about programmes and services when evidence from audience research is used, as it so often is.

Think of recent programmes that you have seen or heard which have left strong and positive memories with you, or have stimulated an interest, led you to new knowledge or understanding or have moved you or touched you in some way. Probably more than one of you are thinking of the same programme, but there would still quite probably be as many programmes chosen as there are people reading this. Most audience research cannot cope with this kind of variety. We have to narrow the field and force you all to make choices so that the results can be summarised easily on a chart of manageable size.

But this is not how we are most likely to highlight the quality and value of broadcasting. The emphasis is mostly on the measurable, especially audience reach,[10] audience share and indices of appreciation — 'A.I.s'. It is true that there are also references to the number of programmes in, or the amount of time devoted to, certain programme genres — education, serious music, poetry, children's programmes, and so on. But none of these singly or collectively provide sufficient measures of value, quality or importance. To answer a question about what in the past year have been the proudest achievements of any part of the BBC, or indeed any private radio or television station, if we are addressing ourselves to the prime purpose of any broadcasting activity, the programmes, we cannot appeal to these ratings alone, not even as the principal means of assessment. We can and do refer to prizes, perhaps to a collection of Sony awards, and of course the critical acclaim of respected writers and critics can be a valid measure of quality. But I am looking for more than these.

Broadcasting involves individual and unique relationships with millions of individuals. The strength and the weakness of research is that it tries to aggregate a multitude of different views, unique patterns of behaviour, personal responses and reactions into generalisations. We try to make sense of the wonderful chaos that is the reality of listening and viewing, by forcing people into categories, percentages and indices. They are all useful in aiding our understanding but they tell only a part of the story. Let me give you an example from my own experience. I was driving home on Whit Sunday evening, 3 June 1990. I was on my own and had to drive some ninety miles from Dorset to my home in Surrey. I turned on the radio. I hadn't planned my listening and hadn't read the *Radio Times*. I cannot remember a time before or since when I have enjoyed an evening's listening so much. I was spoiled for choice. On Radio 3 there was a service from Salisbury Cathedral. On Radio 4 there was a portrait of the Scottish hymn writer and preacher, George Matheson, the author of that old hymn that now seems to have almost disappeared, 'O Love That Will Not Let Me Go'. Later on Radio 4, *Seeds of Faith* featured the Afrikaans poet Bremer Hofmeyr. Radio 2's arts programme had readings by Roger Rees and Virginia McKenna. Radio 1 tempted me with my favourite disc jockey, Andy Kershaw. I listened to some of these all the way through. Others I dipped into for a while. I enjoyed it all immensely and felt that a good part of my annual licence fee had been justified.

---

[10] Reach: the number of people who use any part of the BBC in a week.

What did other listeners do? How many, indeed, listened? Let us look at the ratings.

The audience for any radio is quite small on Sunday evenings. Andy Kershaw was heard by about 0.4% of the population. For George Matheson it was only around 0.3%. *Seeds of Faith's* audience was even smaller at 0.1%. Radio 2's arts programme registered the same, while the service on Radio 3 registered no measured audience at all. Audience measurement is a crude tool. But it does show, I think, that very often we would be in danger of losing programmes of value and quality if we judged them solely on how many listeners they reach. By the way, a 1% audience would be about 500,000 people. None of the programmes reached even half this figure. Here is a question for you to think about. Let us suppose that BBC Radio's Managing Director at that time, David Hatch had scrapped the output on a Sunday evening and replaced it with a schedule which instead attracted many more listeners. This would be regarded as a scheduling success. I wonder if we would regard it as an unqualified success, if the result were to be that we were no longer able to hear programmes of this kind of quality. Of course, what we would all like to see is programmes of quality being listened to or viewed by larger numbers of people!

Before we forget 3 June 1990, I have another observation to make. Some critics mock the BBC for the number of repeats. With riches like these, would there were many more repeats! But I am only one listener; and why should the BBC take account of what I think, especially since I work for them? What I would like to see is a much better way of showing this kind of quality, so that it can be encouraged and guaranteed in the schedules.

That special evening started me thinking about the inadequacies of audience research to reflect these deeper and more difficult-to-measure personal reactions. Now at Bush House we are attempting an experimental way of obtaining insights into the attachments people develop towards international broadcasters. We are looking at the attributes people assign to the BBC in comparison with other broadcasters, to see if they view the BBC as providing, in a superior way, what they are looking for.

We have done this because we feel in IBAR that the measurements are simply not enough to reflect anything like the whole truth about the value of what the BBC produces. We would probably not have embarked on what has become a very expensive and time-consuming research programme, were it not for the pressure we are under in the present climate to measure everything. Without this additional way of assessing value and worth we are left with the simple and bald facts of audience reach and share,[11] and on those figures the fate of much that is worthwhile depends. The press refer to the figures as if they were the only way of assessing the vitality of a radio or television station.

Obviously, it is very important that the BBC should be able to attract large audiences. It is even more important that it should provide everyone with programmes and services they would not want to do without. It should be able to provide programmes that will appeal to all licence payers, so that they will all want to go on providing public support for the continuation of public funding through the licence. But none of this requires that the BBC maintain a high share of listening or viewing. Reach is very important. But what is even more important is those millions of people think of, or do with, what they see and hear. And one measure that will always be of critical importance is: Are the British people prepared to go on supporting the licence fee and paying for the service?

There is another measure often mentioned: the number of hours spent watching television or listening to the radio (counted by service) in a week. In 1994 the average number of hours watched per person in Britain was just over 25 per week. Nearly 11 hours of that was to BBC television, a 43% share. Radio was listened to for just over 16 hours and nearly 8 hours of that was to the BBC — a 49% share. These shares have declined and may continue to do so. But is this necessarily a bad thing for the BBC and a good thing for the new commercial stations? Though it seems generally assumed that it is, I am not so sure. I think that facts such as that within an average week last year about 94% of the British population watched at least some BBC television, and 57% listened to at least some BBC radio, are a better reflection of the service provided.

As a newly appointed BBC manager seventeen years ago I attended one of the famous Uplands courses — a BBC management seminar, where we were asked to carry out an exercise familiar to anybody who attends such courses today. We were asked to prepare a presentation on the theme of what the BBC's response should be to greater competition in commercial radio and television, with the

---

[11] For a description of this research see Mytton, Cooper and Stratton, *op. cit.*

inevitability of satellite delivered services, cable, more private radios and so on. In my syndicate group we put forward such proposals as moving serious or other minority interest programmes to the late evening, developing a soap opera to rival *Coronation Street*, paying more to attract the 'top' disc jockeys, outbidding rival stations to secure major sporting events, and similar ideas of the same kind. We made our presentation to Stephen Hearst, Controller of Radio 3 and then just beginning as Controller of Future Policy. We sat down feeling rather proud of ourselves.

Stephen Hearst was not at all impressed. He questioned all our hidden assumptions. That audience share mattered so much; that minority interests ought to feel privileged to have any of their interests catered to, and should be jolly glad to sit up until all hours to catch the bit of the BBC they really cared about; and (he was particularly scornful of this unquestioning assumption) that increasing audiences, no matter how or what for, was inevitably and always a 'good thing'. Current audience research, he pointed out, showed that the average number of hours watched per person per week in the United Kingdom that year (1978) was eighteen. How would it be a public service to increase that? Would it not be more in the general public interest to make programmes that would stimulate people to switch off and do something else, rather than spend three hours a day in front of the box?

Today the weekly viewing hours standing at twenty-five hours per person, and I think that the Controller of Future Policy had a point. And I take no satisfaction from the fact that the recommendations of our syndicate of wet-behind-the-ears new management trainees were implemented by senior management. I don't claim that it was we who brought *Neighbours* to your screens, nor can we be blamed (or credited) for the absurd fees reportedly being paid to disc jockeys to try to 'save' Radio 1. I do however confess that, unbidden by anyone, we thought of these and other things that have now come to pass. Despite his title, Stephen Hearst, perhaps to our great loss, doesn't seem to have controlled much future policy.

In the World Service, too great an attachment to audience figures could divert our attention from our purpose. Someone once described the BBC as 'Oxfam for the mind'. It is not an adequate description of what we seek to achieve, but there is much truth in it. It is the idea behind the current initiative in Eastern Europe known as the Marshall Plan for the Mind, which involves the BBC making educational programmes for television and radio. The concept is that just as the Marshall Plan provided for some of the urgent economic needs of post-war Europe, these programmes will provide for some of the urgent needs for training and the development of new skills in the post-communist period.

If this is a major part of the BBC's role, we have to be prepared for that role to come to an end. At the moment the BBC has a very large following in Somalia, Nigeria, Burma, Nepal, Iran and many other countries where an 'information Oxfam' is truly needed, either because of existing oppression or a situation of transition towards more freedom. A fall in audiences for the BBC may even therefore be a cause for celebration and rejoicing. A Nepali listener wrote recently:

> When I hear news about Nepal [that] we are unable to hear from Radio Nepal, I feel very pleased. That is the reason I am attracted to your programme and listen every day.

The day will come, we surely hope, when radio and television stations in Nepal, and the press also, will feel free to report these things. The BBC audience will fall, as it fell some years ago, in Greece, Portugal, Spain and Poland as they emerged into the light of greater freedom.

The new management culture that has invaded the public sector in the last few years has produced a mixed harvest. There is much that one can welcome. The greater responsibility for budgeting at the appropriate levels is surely right. It is right that costs should be paid where they are incurred. We now have a system which, when used properly, does tell us what the real costs are of making programmes and broadcasting them. Some money can be saved. Long before Producer Choice was imposed in the World Service, better systems of budgeting produced major savings in many areas, savings which made possible more hours of broadcast, enhanced programmes, more and improved training, more overseas correspondents and other real improvements. This is not, therefore, a full frontal attack on the new management methods.

I do however want to question the priority and prominence given to systems of analysis and assessment which now seem to hold sway. It has been argued that running the BBC is really like doing anything else in the market place. It isn't! A market analogy of broadcasting may work for some of what the BBC does, but the analogy goes too far. Again, I plead guilty here. We made a video about ten years ago about the work of our department and the need for research. At one point the commentary suggested that in some ways, broadcasting was like making and selling baked beans. You need to know about demand and tastes and consumer habits. But this passage in the video, which now makes me wince more than a little, was included merely in order to say something that was very far from the way of thinking at the time; to challenge people to think about the listener as a *kind* of consumer. The consumption of radio programmes is (or we should at least intend it to be) a very different kind of activity from opening and eating a can of beans. The analogy of the market place is, for the most part, inappropriate in the world of broadcasting and public service broadcasting especially.

If we treat the BBC as if it were a commercial enterprise, with marketing plans and product lines, while using the jargon of the market place — 'leveraging the brand' is a phrase I hear too often — we could end up with something that is no different from a commodity, to be bought and sold.

Everywhere in the public sector, the managerialism now in vogue involves systems, measures, indicators, targets and value-for-money exercises. We hear language used which is little different from that used by multi-national companies. We hear less and less about values and human purposes — almost nothing about disinterested public service for its own simple sake. Managing public services more efficiently is an excellent thing to aim for. But it will never be enough. In any public service, the revenue is inelastic. For example, in the BBC making better programmes has to be an end in itself — it won't earn us any more money. So here the marketing analogy breaks down before you get beyond first base. If you are making baked beans you might decide to improve the quality or the packaging in order to attract increased consumption and increase revenue. But there is no market reason for improving programmes in the BBC, nor for that matter, patient care in the health service, and there are several other examples one can think of in the public sector. One problem with Producer Choice could be that forcing producers to work within an internal market place makes them tend to go for the lowest price. They may not of course, but the pressures are in that direction, and all within an organisation which prides itself, and is valued by its viewers and listeners throughout the world, for the quality of what it does. Could the BBC have built something within itself that will lead to its own destruction? We must all fervently hope not. But we also have to recognise the dangers.

One of the weapons that public service broadcasters must keep to hand at all times is a conviction about why they broadcast at all. The philosophy and ethos must be shared. I believe it is, and very strongly too, in the World Service. I am sure that it is our greatest strength. There is a shared philosophy and sense of purpose, expressed very well in that vision statement I read earlier. The BBC exists as a public good. It wasn't created to be, in the words of one BBC document I read recently, 'a big player'. There is nothing wrong with being successful, but being big in the world is not an end in itself. It is the consequence of what we do, not the goal.

The BBC is already 'a big player' for reasons that have nothing to do with ownership, number of employees, number of affiliates or cross-media partnerships, and have everything to do with the quality of what it does, its independence from commercial and political control and, above all, how it is perceived by those it seeks to serve. And of course it does have a lot to do with the fact that it has the largest audience for any international radio service. But this is a result of the quality of what it provides, not a *measure* of that quality.

Our purpose, at least in public service broadcasting, should be to hold broad public support. This will be achieved and sustained by making programmes that delight, surprise, sometimes even infuriate, give a sense of community despite differences between us, and have different appeals to a wide range of tastes, interests and outlooks. How is this to be done at a time when the whole ecology of broadcasting is changing into something quite different? The new technologies are beginning to allow much more individual choice. But people also want to share something in common, something which is universal, a sense of community which the BBC is supreme at providing. It is significant that the BBC always enjoys the greatest national share of audience in Britain when it comes to coverage of the great national events, like the 1995 VE-Day celebrations. Interestingly, it is a feature of the World Service which so attracts many listeners world-wide. They express their appreciation of a service which makes them feel a part of a world community of shared problems and shared delights.

I may have sounded very gloomy about the portents. Actually I am not, I am an optimist. A few days ago I was privileged to attend the annual James Cameron memorial lecture, the same event at which John Tusa spoke last year and gave the speech to which I referred when we began. Before an audience of press and radio journalists, the annual James Cameron award was announced. It went this year to George Alagiah, the BBC's Southern Africa correspondent. He was deservedly praised for his skill in getting challenging or difficult stories, especially about the Third World and its problems, past 'ratings-bitten' new editors. So I am not claiming that the ratings rule at all times. But often quality and worthwhile material has to fight too hard to be heard. The point is, I think, that we now too often underestimate, rather than overestimate, the capacity, interests and tastes of our audiences. This has already happened in the popular press, as illustrated that evening in the James Cameron memorial lecture given by Jeremy Isaacs, when he showed how journalism in the old *Daily Mirror* and *Daily Herald*, forerunner of today's *Sun*, was often of a quality rarely seen in popular journalism now. Is the same downward trend now happening in television and radio? I still hope not.

It will I hope be clear by now that I see a strong moral dimension to the current debate about management in the public service. It is a connection especially strong in broadcasting, which is a powerful form of human communication. Like all forms of communication it can be a force for good or evil and of the extremes of both. One of the many evils of Nazism was its promotion, through broadcasting and the press, of utterly false and perverted values. One of the greatest good things that anyone can do for another is to speak the truth, especially when to do so is dangerous and life threatening. Some of the worst forms of cruelty and wickedness ever committed have been committed against people for what they say.

When we talk about broadcasting, a major form of human communication, we are talking about something that really matters. It is at, or near to, the heart of things. So I don't find making a specifically Christian connection at all difficult or awkward. It is implicit in the theme of quality in public service, which seems to me to be very much a matter of right and wrong, of true and false values, of a choice between mere appearance or true reality.

I am reminded of Paul's criticism of Christians who continued to look for outward appearances rather than consider inner realities in themselves and others. This was at the heart of Jesus' teaching and his obvious deep dislike of hypocrisy. There are many examples in the Bible of the use of false or inappropriate measures or assessments of value. Perhaps the oddest one is in the second book of Samuel, when David carried out a census. The writer assumes that we all realise immediately why this was wrong and doesn't trouble to tell us why. It is more or less the same story in the equivalent passage in the first book of Chronicles.

> Satan rose up against Israel and incited David to take a census of Israel. So David said to Joab and the commanders of the troops, 'Go and count the Israelites from Beersheba to Dan. Then report back to me so that I may know how many there are.'
>
> But Joab replied, 'May the Lord multiply his troops a hundred times over. My lord the king, are they not all my lord's subjects? Why does my lord want to do this? Why should he bring guilt on Israel?'[12]

But David insisted, and the writer goes on to report that the command was evil in the sight of God who punished Israel. And it is recorded that David saw the error of his ways and repented.

Why was this such an obviously wrong thing to do? There was no religious prohibition on censuses. Moses numbered the people when in the wilderness. But this was for a clear purpose — to list all the men over twenty who were fit for military service. The Levites were excluded because they were exempt as priests. They were counted separately and with a different purpose. The point of the story seems to be that David was counting his people for a vainglorious purpose. He had been successful in battle against Israel's enemies. But now his pride, the arrogance of absolute power and thinking that he knew best, required him, in his own view, to count his achievements and measure his power. It was perhaps an obsession with the numbers which reflected glory on David rather than with the underlying story of God's blessing of Israel.

It can be the same in audience research and the way in which we use the measures we obtain. We are now in danger of spending more time and putting more emphasis on these and other performance indicators than on the defining purpose of all our activities. One can say the same about other areas of life. In the health service, in education and in public transport and other services we seem to have elevated measures of things that are consequences not the main purpose of the activity.

When preparing for this lecture over the last few months, I have been amazed how often this theme has confronted me. In many ways

---
[12] 1 Chronicles 21:1–3.

I have been encouraged by the frequency with which I have come across challenging remarks and discussions in the press and in recently published books. It seems that more and more people are beginning to see the false priorities that have been assigned to so much human activity, whether it is Members of Parliament questioning the closure on economic grounds of yet more hospitals, or commentators in the press pointing to the value-laden (and false values at that) assumptions behind such apparently neutral things as economic indicators. We are seeing an increasing number of books, both here and across the Atlantic which employ these themes and question the prevailing orthodoxies. There are many examples, but I would particularly mention Will Hutton's book *The State We're In*, the Henley Centre's *After the Gold Rush* and from America, *The Good Society*.[13]

What are the defining sentences that would express today what the BBC is for? Will the World Service's statement of purpose suffice? Probably it won't, because of its emphasis in a global context on news and information. There is another sentence that greets you in the entrance to Broadcasting House. Malcolm Muggeridge quoted from it in his opening lecture.

> This temple of the arts and muses is dedicated to Almighty God by the first governors of broadcasting in the year 1931, Sir John Reith being Governor General. It is their prayer that good seeds sown may bring forth a good harvest, that all things hostile to peace or purity may be banished from this house, that the people, inclining their ears to whatsoever things are beautiful, honest and of good report, may tread the paths of wisdom and righteousness.

Muggeridge comments wryly that it was

> a good thing that the words are in Latin and not in English! Otherwise, for decency's sake, they would have to be removed, or, like the seven commandments in Orwell's *Animal Farm*, adjusted.[14]

Well, they haven't been removed, and I hope they never will be. I also hope that the inspiration of our founders, however quaint those words may now sound, still has some resonance and meaning today.

There is another aspect of public service today that I find distasteful and which has emerged from the same fashion for an

---

[13] Will Hutton, *The State We're In* (Jonathan Cape, 1995); Stewart Lansley, *After the Gold Rush* (The Henley Centre, 1994); Robert N. Bellah and others, *The Good Society* (Vintage Books, NY, 1992).

[14] Muggeridge, op. cit. p.26.

inappropriate management culture. It is the way that employment within the public service has been made little different from any job anywhere. What should motivate us as broadcasters committed to public service? As Christians we are taught to give unconditionally, as Jesus Christ did. In public service we should also give unconditionally. The principle of service is what should motivate us, not financial gain, nor power, nor influence, nor national glory. I was reminded of this just a few weeks ago when the Chief Constable of Hampshire Police, John Hoddinott, said that he would refuse a new fixed-term appointment that carried with it a significant element of performance-related pay. This is what he wrote to fellow police officers.

> I joined the police out of a sense of public service ... recognising the financial disadvantage. Had I wanted the principles of the market-place, I would not have made that decision ... The notion that I will work harder or more effectively because of performance related pay is absurd and objectionable, if not insulting.

Stuart Steven, writing with joyous approval of this in the *Evening Standard* used these words:

> Hallelujah and hosanna, a public servant has spoken out against one of the great heresies of the modern age — that everybody and everything can be assessed by the strict operation of the market-place and that nothing that cannot be measured in strict cash terms is worthwhile. [15]

I have the audacity to hope that thoughts like these will begin to turn the tide, so that in the public service of broadcasting, if not elsewhere also, we will at least sometimes turn the title of this lecture around and say with faith and conviction: 'Never mind the ratings, feel the quality!'

---

[15] *Evening Standard* 25 April 1995

4: The Age of Information

Alan Rogers

THE ELECTRONIC CLASSROOM?

Education is a curious part of broadcasting. Attitudes towards it from within the business are ambivalent, to say the least. On the one hand producers are pleased to be able occasionally to say that their work is educational — it somehow gives a greater feeling of permanence to know that it will be remembered and used after the brief moment of transmission. On the other hand they dismiss educational output as being marginal to the real business of mass broadcasting, because it is targeted at a classroom or a particular group of adults.

I remember feeling that ambiguity myself when I was working for the mainstream audiences of Radio 1 and Radio 4. Somehow the people in Schools or Continuing Education departments were half broadcaster, half teacher — earnest people, aping the language of proper broadcasters but concerned with strange things like the intellectual development of their listeners.

I recall feeling rather generous when I invited the Education Department to share a peak-time phone-in with my team. I thought myself very enlightened to do so, although truth to tell part of my motivation was that my wife was working in BBC Education and I therefore knew the producers to be perfectly OK people.

Later, when I became head first of the Television Schools Department and then the Adult Education Department, I experienced exactly the same phenomenon from the other side. The Head of Drama or the Head of Sport were great friends and colleagues, but somehow you knew that when the chips were down they felt that they were doing the really important job — and that education was just one of the things which the BBC did because it was the BBC!

In one sense there is a good reason for this ambiguity. It has to do with the fundamental purposes of general broadcasting and of educational broadcasting. One exists to inform or entertain large audiences at a fairly superficial level (although there are exceptions); the other exists to influence a smaller number of people much more deeply.

It's not just to do with *size of audience* — some of the programmes under the education banner have reached massive numbers — but has more to do with intention and the way in which one *uses* the medium of television or radio. If you are truly using television to develop skills and knowledge, to give deeper understanding or influence attitudes, then it is an altogether different undertaking from producing *Top Gear* or *A Question of Sport*.

It is indeed the *objectives* of a series which make it educational rather than general. If the prime intention is to help the viewer to acquire a set of skills, or to understand context in a logical way or to generate understanding systematically, then the series is educational. If it is to inform in passing, or to give some brief context on the wing in the course of a journalistic exercise, then the programme has other goals.

Bear in mind that there is a difference between acquiring information and being educated. Information and knowledge are not the same. One might say that knowledge is 'information with attitude', that knowledge is partly build up of information that has been processed and shaped and framed to be educational. Roaming the Internet picking up random information is not educational. Education needs structure and meaning.

What is fascinating is that whatever the ambiguous feelings between general and educational broadcaster, the generalist has been very quick to borrow the best developments in education. It is commonplace now for many programmes to offer fact sheets after the programme. This was entirely the development of educational broadcasters keen to extend the learning opportunities. Telephone help lines came from the same source. The first aid classes offered by *999* had been preceded ten years before by the same thing with an educational series called *Save a Life*. Broadcasting Support Services, of which I am a trustee, developed from a single educational initiative into an organisation employing 150 people to support programmes on every channel be they dramas, factual programmes or entertainment with books, help lines and print of every description.

THE PUBLIC

The view of those in broadcasting is one thing, that of the audience, quite another. My own experience is that there is vast appreciation and goodwill around the country for the work of educational broadcasters. It really does make a difference to teachers wrestling to focus the interest and attention of either noisy eight-year-olds or fifteen-year-olds who want to leave school and earn a living as quickly as possible.

Similarly there are an astonishing number of people you meet who thank you with metaphorical tears in their eyes for this or that adult education series which provoked a new interest, or had some profound effect on their lives. In fact all the studies show that the majority of people want and expect the BBC and Channel 4 to provide a good range of educational output. The Reithian trinity of 'information, entertainment and education' lives on. The public demands education from the television screen, even if they don't personally consume it in its purest form very often. They like to feel it is available.

Many pieces of research exist which demonstrate that education is something expected of broadcasters — and especially the BBC.

There's a challenge here for the broadcasters which I think on the whole has been very well met in Britain — namely to provide entertaining general output which has a genuinely educational side. I'm talking here not only about educational broadcasting itself but also about the many factual shows — from wildlife to science to documentary and social drama — which leave you better informed or challenged in your perception of the world. We have the public service tradition of broadcasting in Britain to thank for that. It certainly is possible to make programmes which are both educational and entertaining; and I think it is true to say that both BBC and Channel 4 are concentrating on doing that as a matter of deliberate policy right now.

Indeed before I left the BBC we started the process known as 'commissioning out' which continues now. It involves commissioning educational output from subject specialists in other programme departments, thus using the BBC's expertise to the full. The gap between education and general output is closing — or to put it another way, it is in the BBC's interest to emphasise its educational role in as much of its output as possible.

However there is perhaps another factor at work here. In our preparations for ARK2, the new Christian television station with which I am concerned, we have thought long and hard about why so many people believe in a God but utterly reject the notion of organised religion. A survey carried out for us by NOP, showed that 71% of the population believe in a being beyond themselves, however defined. 64% believe there is a spiritual void in this country, and no fewer than 79% believe that Christianity has something to offer to fill this void in terms of values and morals. This is to me an astounding finding. What a fund of goodwill! Yet compare that to the English Church Census figure of 10% of the adult population in church each Sunday — 15% at best — who might call themselves regular church-goers.

Why don't people interested in Christian ideas and values go to church?

Could the answer be less to do with the actual message of the Christian faith than with the institutions and authority — emblems with which Christianity is bound up in this country? Are people rejecting authority and institutions, rather than the kernel of Christianity when considered at a more personal level? In Britain today discussion of morals and values often takes place through the medium of soap operas! It does not happen in religious broadcasting, at least not for most people. It is in *Eastenders* and *Brookside* that most people get to discuss what is right and wrong and to pick over people's motivations and decisions.

There is a mirror for this in the way education is best delivered by television to the general adult population these days. Although there are exceptions such as the Open University and language courses, most adult education is carried out almost accidentally. The educational broadcaster creeps up on the adult viewer as he or she sits sprawled in their armchair, with hopefully a good educational experience! In other words, not many adults opt positively for a formal course but they are happy to accept interesting educational experiences when they come unbidden.

In education and religion alike, the process goes on informally and naturally. It is no longer to do with formal process, be it college or church. This is not only because of a suspicion of formality and structures; it is also connected with what is empowering for the individual and what fits naturally with his or her life at a particular time. Perhaps another way to put it is that religion or education flow from their need rather than a sense of obligation.

TECHNOLOGY

But whatever the ambiguity surrounding educational broadcasting professionally, and however much the public likes it, one fact is clear in these days of rapid technological change. Keith Yeomans put it very well when he wrote recently: 'Education has been the unassailable banner at the vanguard of every electronic assault on the way we share ideas.'

Education is the justification given for each development, the reason we should buy the new-fangled wireless, television, video, CD-ROM, interactive equipment or whatever it is. Right at the beginning of radio was schools broadcasting. Now education even more than entertainment is the reason given for interactivity in the home, just as it once was for home computers. Will this actually be true — or once parents have purchased CDi or CD-ROM, will education give way to entertainment in the software actually used?

Now of course education is motherhood and apple pie; education is said to be the answer to many of the ills which beset our world from the population explosion in the developing world to the underskilled workforce we have here in Britain. Call me an optimist, but I believe that the new media with their great promise of interactivity really do potentially herald a new age of learning in which the learner has control, and can alter the context and control the pace to his or her personal understanding.

BASIC FACTS

First, though, a few basic facts about the existing electronic classroom. Britain is blessed with the best two school television services in the world, and I say that on the basis of a great deal of experience of school television around the world. In a sense it is a triumph for competition. Because the BBC did it well, ITV, and now Channel 4, have had to maintain their own standards and have also provided a first-class service.

The result is that you would be very hard put to find a school in Britain that does not use television as part of its regular learning pattern. The greatest use is in the primary schools. In the infant classes they still watch it live, or listen to *Music and Movement* or join in with the radio assembly for worship. Some favourite series such as *Watch* or *Words and Pictures* get audiences of between one and two million children.

As you go up the age range, more programmes are recorded and used when they fit into the teachers' plans. In the secondary schools all use is recorded. Often quite short clips from educational programmes or mainstream programmes which teachers have spotted during their personal viewing of programmes such as *Tomorrow's World* or *Life in the Freezer* are used to illustrate a teaching point.

This is partly connected with the provision of hardware. The typical primary school still has only one or two television sets and one VCR, whereas most secondary schools would have perhaps fifteen or twenty televisions and recorders. Indeed at the secondary level departments tend to have their own equipment with Geography, English and History departments being the biggest users, followed by science and PSE, with the Maths departments bringing up the rear.

This is not surprising when you look at the things which television can do which the teacher cannot. Teachers cannot for example transport the children to Africa or Japan to study the geography and people of those lands; they cannot put on dramas or use historical newsreel or actuality footage. They cannot in science use X-ray techniques to look inside an animal or slow their movement down with slow motion. On the other hand mathematics is a conceptual subject which is difficult to bring alive on television.

A good teacher will not use television as an interlude but will work hard to integrate it as a motivator, to inspire and involve the class. It is invaluable too in a number of subjects — especially RE and personal and social education — to offer case studies, role models and dramas which open up difficult areas.

At the adult level formal education, as I have indicated, does not take centre stage although the Open University is a world-class institution which has been much copied and still leads in many fields, including the educational use of interactive media. The Open Business School has a huge membership in central and eastern Europe, as those countries come to terms with the reality of a market economy. Also on general television there are increasing numbers of programmes — especially in languages and training — which are used by the rapidly expanding Further Education colleges.

Nevertheless the main focus of education for adults is pitched to meet people in their armchairs in front of their television sets. After all, television is a mass medium and the justification for using it for education is that you reach people where they are, with material which will enrich their lives. For this reason continuing education programmes look like, and are made to the same production values as, general output. They have to win their place in a peak-time schedule and do so much more often these days.

The key difference of intention requires the educational broadcaster to be supported by education officers (as will the schools producers) whose job is to define the learning needs of the audience and to work with the producer to structure a programme series to meet those needs. There is great art in this. All educational broadcasting has a large infrastructure of consultancy groups and advisers to make sure that the right learning needs are being addressed in the right way at the right time.

A recent (as of 1995) literacy campaign on BBC 1 illustrates good targeting. The plan was to reach poor readers who are themselves now parents of young children — all the research shows that the children of poor readers tend to be themselves poor readers. If the parents can be helped to have the confidence to work with their children on reading then both benefit. The Americans call such an arrangement a 'double-duty dollar'.

Our partner was the Adult Literary Basic Skills Unit, which is part of the Department of Education. We chose as our vehicle a thirty-second advertisement made by Bartle, Bogle and Hegarty — the first time BBC output had been made by an advertising agency. Very wide educational research was carried out and the result was that no fewer than 314,000 people called the help line. Allowing for people who do not follow through, that is still a very large number of parents helped to have the confidence to read with their children — a simple thing that most of us probably take for granted. The point is that using the mass madia with clear educational objectives and good targeting has a very powerful effect.

FUTURE USE

So much for how educational output is used now. How will it be when interactivity really gets going? At the moment, only about 30%

of secondary schools, and virtually no primary schools, have CD-ROM players.

Of course the basic point is that you will get random-access computer or cable screen and on-demand services, rather than ones scheduled by the men and women at Television Centre. David Puttnam, the film producer who is currently involved in trying to set up a World University Network with the BBC and British Council, pointed out recently that television and radio work best for education when both teacher and learner are mature in their use of them. With the new interactivity the teacher is not so much a deliverer of education as an entrepreneur of open learning — learning controlled by the learner. The barriers of home, work and school or college come down and the student can make his or her own mix. Learner power is the key; control for the individual, all-important.

Puttnam points out that the media are at the core of our new society with its emphasis on knowledge, information and learning. The possible long-term fusion of television with fibre-optic and computer-based technologies has implications which are stunning. And of course given that English is the dominant world language, there is a huge opportunity for our own educators and media people. Not only do the majority of the world's books and films use English, it is also a language which is used by almost a billion people as their second language.

Given all this, surprisingly little research has been done into how people actually learn by the electronic media. An honourable exception among media researchers is Di Laurillard of the Open University, who has carried out research on narrative (used by most programmes) and the amount of screen time taken up in Open University programmes by main point, subsidiary point and examples. Not surprisingly, it revealed that the more time given to the main point, the better that learners remembered it.

This, though, holds true for ordinary linear television programmes. For multi-media learning packages the situation is very different in terms of narrative because of the learner's control. He or she does not use the material in a pre-determined order. This undermines narrative, so how do learners recognise the main point?

Laurillard points out that with interactive, the learner can test and compare with the teacher's narrative (which will still have authority but will be tested and questioned) and suggests four stages. Learners need:

1. To discuss, react to the expert's presentation and articulate their version, perhaps through essays, and get an expert to react to that.
2. To act, investigate with a goal and get feedback.
3. To adapt according to their understanding.
4. To reflect, digest and develop understanding.

All of this needs a variety of media — perhaps television to present first-hand testimony or expert opinion, video and workbook support so that the learner goes at his or her own pace, and multimedia to act with feedback.

Both Channel 4 and BBC are responding to the challenge of multimedia with many new learning packages and commercial products. BBC Education is now, for example, producing CD-ROM, CDi, laser disks, books, videos, audio materials and pamphlets. It has set up the BBC Bulletin Board and the Networking Club on the Internet. In the future we will see the television series and the associated discs and print all piped down the same fibre-optic cable to be received in the school as a package. This is a logical follow-on of the importance which educational broadcasting has always given to follow-up opportunities to help the learning progress further.

People speak of 'the learning society'. And so it is. In a situation where knowledge is the driver, we need a learning home, a learning workplace and a learning community. The prizes go to those who are flexible and responsive to change and new need. Gone are the days of heavy authority and slow-moving institutions. Now a facilitating and learning spirit is what works best. The new media are ideally suited to this approach.

VALUES

But whose values are transmitted? Does television transmit a narrow agenda of values? Are those values out of touch with the majority?

The true answer, in my view, is that television and radio both reflect and lead. Reflect, in the sense that they cannot get too far away from the concensus of society or they will lose their audience base. But lead, in the sense that has been true right from Lord Reith, that public service broadcasting must serve the public by sometimes showing it a higher vision.

A recent example of this might be the issue of equal opportunities. I think it is undoubtedly true that both off-screen and on-screen the broadcasters have been ahead of society in dealing fairly with women, members of ethnic minorities and disabled people. I am certainly not saying that the present performance is perfect — if you took your cue from television you would believe that only a tiny proportion of the British population is elderly, for example — but it has been distinctly ahead of public opinion and has suffered the accusation of being overly 'politically correct'.

That is an example of the broadcasters coaxing opinion forward. A reverse example might be the way our screens accurately reflect the greed and acquisitive aspects of our society. Witness the emphasis on the National Lottery, upon game shows and the kind of moral judgments used in shows like *Do the Right Thing*. The broadcasters have to reflect as well as to lead, as Robert McLeish demonstrated much more fully in the first lecture in this series.

Education is an example of leading. It emphasises the liberation of knowledge, understanding and new skills. It empowers people and helps them not only to determine to take a more pro-active approach to their own affairs but also to open their minds to other influences, other cultures, other possibilities. Given the huge importance of the media in our society, they play an essential part in the essential process of education for the majority of our people.

If the range of values shown is more narrow than that of society then we are likely to see that remedied as cable and satellite expand. The much greater range of ownership and editorial stance must have an impact on the fairly liberal consensus values portrayed at present.

CHRISTIAN EDUCATION

I want to conclude with some ideas and challenges about Christian education.

The church which set out so vigorously in Victorian times to educate children in the faith through the Sunday School movement — the same church which had been the instigator and inspiration of education from medieval times — has somehow lost some of its vision for education beyond the school gate.

Within school both Catholics and Anglicans have been steadfast in maintaining their commitment to education and also in adapting their approach to a very different kind of society. It is worth noting that around a third of all primary schools in Britain are church schools. There are major problems to do with religious education and school worship which are yet to be resolved; but these are much more numerous in the purely state sector.

But beyond school, at home, in church and in society in general, one does not detect so much concern among Christians. And yet, children are growing up within a secular culture where they often have no sense of the transcendent at all; where, if they go to one of many ordinary state schools, they will seldom get any impression of anything beyond the material, physical world around them. Certainly they would not glean a clue about who Moses was; and as for Noah, they wouldn't know him from Adam! So even at the level of ordinary discourse, references to feeding the 5,000 or to the good Samaritan would leave them puzzled.

Can it be good for generations of children to lack these cultural and spiritual frames of reference? A world in which people have never had the possibility of their minds being opened to something beyond their own self-interest is surely an appalling prospect! No wonder ignorance rules when it comes to religion. One of the tenets of Willow Creek, the American church which lays so much stress on appealing to the unchurched, is that although people may be ill-informed about Christianity, they are also uninformed about their own self-invented creeds!

What is the church doing to alleviate this situation? What is it doing to campaign against it, particularly in the church itself? You could reply 'But we have updated Sunday Schools to Junior Church' — and it is true that at the last count 14% of the nation's children are to be found in church on any Sunday, compared to 10% of the adults I mentioned earlier.

But is the stress on learning or on belonging? Is learning really happening, or is it a matter of child-minding — and never mind about being too tough, because the children might choose not to come back? One has the greatest sympathy. Children tend to drop out of church from the age when they could really get down to some serious learning about Christianity. But is this good enough?

In the United States most churches have adult education classes before or after worship so that people can make a morning of it; both worship and learning. Here we do not have that emphasis, and young people sense the values and the kind of culture they are in. Fundamentally education is not high enough on the agenda of church people. They do not understand or support Christian teachers enough, they do not lobby for religious education enough — they have too many other things on their plate. This is not the case with our Muslim brothers and sisters. They regard education as of first-rate importance to the confessing community. Let me make it clear that I am not suggesting we should try to behave as if Britain were a dominantly Christian country, where everyone is obliged to study the faith dogmatically. But I am suggesting that we campaign to cherish and draw out the spiritual dimension of all children, through appropriately Christian and multi-faith education.

It has always surprised me that existing religious broadcasting places such a small emphasis on children. Children and television go together like ham and eggs!

I mentioned earlier the newly announced Christian television channel ARK2 which, it is planned, will begin broadcasting nationally in 1996. We were delighted to get such a huge response to our launch. It tends to support the basic argument that in Britain there is huge latent interest in morals, values and belief. (Incidentally, the negative impact of televangelism cuts deep. We found ourselves having to explain again and again that we are totally unlike the popular conception of a hard-preaching channel which is always appealing for money.)

In our research we talked to young people of course, and in support of what I have been arguing they said that religion had dropped from their agenda outside school; and now that they are a little older, it is unfashionable in their peer group. The mothers, however, were quite unambiguous in their desire for their children to have a good Christian education. There is a great desire for children to have a framework of values and principles.[1]

ARK2 will have a very broad range of output which will include music and entertainment, but there will very definitely be education

---

[1] Incidentally vocabulary is enormously important in reaching out to non-church people with matters of morals and values. We were told very firmly not to call the channel a religious one! Here for interest is a list of words which are OK: Moral, Christian, God, Debate. Here are some which are dodgy: Religious, Worship, Evangelist, Born again, Preach, Spiritual. And here are some which are neutral: Bible, Church, Comparative Religion.

for both children and adults. On most days there will be programmes which unpack the faith and show what it says and how it is applied. And there will be weekend programmes for children at home which are educational.

However perhaps the most innovative part of our plans, due to start in 1997, is to open up each morning with material for school worship. No one other than BBC Radio does this and yet it is an area where teachers have maximum difficulty. Fundamentally they lack the skills — and in many cases the inclination — to handle classroom worship; yet the current legislation asks for mainly Christian worship assembly to be conducted every day. Setting aside the question of whether this demand is unreasonable for older children, it is certainly impractical for many individual teachers, who need help. Our plan is to offer suitable material for all four Key Stages; in the case of younger children, actual broadcast assemblies, and in the case of older children, the kind of personal case study which gets debate going in the classroom. Naturally all the appropriate print back-up will be available.

This is the kind of project which the Secretary of State for Education is keen to support. Indeed her department has asked for input on its ultimate success, because they want to exploit the superhighways of education. That of course includes cable television in the classroom. ARK2 is also exploring ways in which it can enrich the resources for religious education available to schools. These are already provided to some degree by BBC Television and Channel 4, whereas resources for worship are not.

The challenge to Christians is to use all possible means of educating both children and adults about what Christianity actually is. No one else is going to do it for us.

5: Religious Broadcasting — For the Nation or the Ghetto?

Tim Dean

Any discussion of religious broadcasting in Britain must start with its context: and that context is one of public service broadcasting (PSB). So I want to begin with a brief look at public service broadcasting, and then within that culture the place of religious broadcasting; and lastly the rise of the 'new' confessional broadcasting. I will conclude by comparing the two.

PUBLIC SERVICE BROADCASTING IN THE UK

Let us begin by looking at the public service broadcasting environment — which, as Bob McLeish has already reminded us (p.3), has as its primary purpose to serve the audience and the community, and not, for example, to make money or accumulate wealth and power.

Context

In Britain public service broadcasting is neither a static nor an inflexible institution. It is an ideal. It started, with what is now called 'The First Age of Broadcasting', with radio and the formation of the BBC (which had until then been a company) as a corporation.

It is important to recognise that public service broadcasting has been publicly debated for decades and constantly adapted to the changing character of our society and of the broadcasting ecology. It has not been set in concrete, but is open to change and modification. The most notable change was the arrival of independent television, introducing a commercial dimension to our broadcasting culture. Then came BBC2, which widened the breadth of television particularly in regard to minority interests, and initially to what might be described as 'worthy' programming; and Channel 4 (S4C in Wales), in which the broadcaster acted as a publisher whose specific brief was to find alternative programming to fill the gaps left by the mainstream channels. The fourth channels also added a further emphasis on minority interests. Another expansion of the role of public service broadcasting is reflected in the history of radio, with the expansion of BBC national, regional and local services and the setting up of Independent Local Radio.

Characteristics

Thus the ideal which is public service broadcasting has developed over a period of time, and now has four main characteristics:

An independent public service. Public service broadcasting in Britain is intended to be independent from political pressures; the government should not interfere editorially or dictate programme content. And it is relatively independent from commercial pressures. Although ITV carries advertising, this has been regulated since ITV's inception. Advertising can occupy only a certain number of minutes in each hour, and the difference between programming and advertising must be made clear (which is why in Britain advertising slots are introduced by phrases like 'End of Part One', whereas in American television commercials often break into programmes arbitrarily and without notice). Commercial sponsorship of programmes was prohibited in Britain until recently, but even though today, for example, *Inspector Morse* is sponsored by Beamish Stout and the 'ITV Movies' series by Diet Coke, such sponsors are not supposed to influence editorial policy. So UK public service broadcasting is dual-funded, by the BBC licence fee and by commercial funding of ITV and Channel 4.

A commitment to every member of our national communities. A second element of the public service broadcasting ideal is that almost everyone is able to receive transmissions: rural dwellers, as well as their more easily reached urban counterparts, are provided with a broadcast service.

Artistic and creative freedom. Thirdly, programme producers are given artistic and creative freedom within broad boundaries, and where required they seek to attain 'political balance'.

Variety in programming. Lastly, public service broadcast programming represents a wide variety of programme types, unlike 'narrow-casting' channels such as MTV and Eurosport. A key purpose of public service broadcasting is summed up in the old Independent Broadcasting Authority charter, which stated that the IBA licensed the ITV companies to 'provide television services as a public service for disseminating information, education and entertainment'; programmes 'shall maintain a proper and wide range in their subject matter'. The purpose of public service broadcasting (which can be traced back to the era of John Reith) is to inform, educate and entertain, and to provide variety.

But the concept of wide-ranging broadcasting means something quite specific. It means a wide range of *topics* and *subject* areas, such as sport, drama, news, current affairs, religion, arts, music, etc. It does not mean (from an editorial perspective) a wide range of *different voices* from the divergent range of social groups, ideologies and cultures found in British society today. It is important to understand that the 'wide variety' to which public service broadcasting subscribes is a variety of genre, not of ideology or culture.

These basic editorial parameters and values of public service broadcasting have been achieved by what some believe to be an evil word: 'regulation' (or, if you prefer, 'legislation'). If we want to understand the basic building blocks of public service broadcasting, we must become familiar with some other related key terms, such as 'safeguards', and the role of the public service broadcaster as a 'gatekeeper': a body which acts on behalf of the general public and has a role in determining what audiences shall and shall not see or hear.

Regulation in this context has two specific attributes. One is *prescriptive* — what public service broadcasters must do (for example, carry a wide range of programming). The other is proscriptive — what they cannot and must not do (for example, transmit programmes that incite racial hatred, allow religious groups to use air-time to fund-raise, etc.).

I believe that regulation is very important to broadcasting culture. It is not something to be feared, but something to be valued. However, not everybody agrees, and certainly not all Christians agree, particularly in America. David W. Clark, Dean of the College of Communication of Arts of Regent University, Virginia Beach, observes,

The PSB model assumes that there are prudent and even-handed broadcasting regulators who act as fiduciaries for the public. Inherent in this model is the assumption that these regulators will turn to programmers who are trustworthy, competent, fair and in some way representative of the main viewpoints within the population on a given topic. They take upon themselves to determine not just what the audience wants but what they believe the audience ought to see and hear. Thus the regulators and programmers assume a very powerful gatekeeper role for audiences.[1]

David Clark has been President of the National Religious Broadcasters, and Regent University is part of Pat Robertson's empire that includes CBN (Christian Broadcasting Network). I quote him because there are many Christians who argue similarly. Yet is it not true that every broadcaster, including the major US networks and including Pat Robertson's CBN, makes choices about what in their opinion the audience ought to see and not see, hear and not hear? That is not so much an argument against public service broadcasting as a self-evident fact. The real questions are: Who is making the decisions about what viewers and listeners will receive? To whom are they accountable? And in whose interests are those decisions made?

David Clark's approach exemplifies the spurious argument that freedom and regulation are opposites, that what is unregulated is free. I suggest that the reverse is the case; that the regulated public service broadcasting model in Britain has provided greater freedom, not less. It has given greater freedom for voices in the whole of our society to be heard. It also gives a greater freedom in terms of choice of programming, because it is required not to produce, for example, endless soap opera through the day, but must ensure coverage of news, drama, sport, music, etc.

So I believe that we have a lot to thank public service broadcasting for. It has a number of key virtues. Regulation has protected radio and television from the possible worst excesses of commercial and political exploitation (and indeed religious exploitation); it has provided a wide range of types of programming; it has maintained the routine production of high-quality programmes; and public service broadcasting can make sure that the marginalised and the poor can be heard, as well as minority cultures and interests.

---

[1] David W. Clark, 'The Public Interest', in: Peter Elvy (ed.), *Opportunities and Limitations in Religious Broadcasting* (Pub. for the Jerusalem Trust by the Centre for Theology & Public Issues, University of Edinburgh, 1991), p.110.

However, it does have limitations and deficiencies, for a perfect broadcasting model does not exist. Public service broadcasting does have a tendency to marginalise the interests and perspectives of minorities, who cannot always mobilise the resources to set up their own 'confessional' (for example Christian, Jewish or Muslim) broadcasting stations. Public service broadcasting outlets have done much to try to rectify this, but they are still not very comfortable with minority groups and minority interests within our society. Winston Churchill said that the sign of a civilised society is one that takes due care of its minorities — and that due care is an important building block of democracy.

Public service broadcasting is also susceptible to institutional bias, for example in its treatment of political and trade union issues, as the authors of *Bad News, More Bad News* and *Really Bad News* have ably demonstrated. Another key deficiency is that sometimes in pursuing 'balance', impartiality becomes a lack of commitment.

Bob McLeish has already reminded us that broadcasting should speak to the whole person — and, by extension, it should reflect the diversity of the whole community. And religion plays a major part in that. We cannot understand public service religious broadcasting, if we do not have some basic knowledge of what public service broadcasting is about in the first place.

The development of religious broadcasting

The first advisory committee ever appointed by the BBC was the Religious Advisory Committee (1923). Its composition meant that the public service broadcasting model reflected, right from the start, an embryonic ecumenism. Of its three members, one was an Anglican priest, one was a Presbyterian minister and the third was a Roman Catholic layman. The committee rapidly expanded, to include representatives of the nonconformist churches of England and Wales. Right at the outset a decision was made that religious broadcasting in the public service arena was not going to be aligned, or indeed established, with any one church denomination. Now the stated aims of BBC religious broadcasting are these:

> To seek to reflect the worship, thought and action of the principal religious traditions represented in the UK, recognising that those traditions are mainly, but not exclusively Christian. To seek to provide to viewers and listeners those beliefs, ideas, issues and experiences in the

contemporary world which are evidently related to a religious interpretation of life. And to seek to meet the religious interests, concerns and needs of those on the fringe of, or outside, the organized life of religious bodies.

There is no legal requirement for the BBC to produce religious programmes. However, within the general remit for public service broadcasting, the BBC recognises that religion is an important part of life, and therefore the Corporation has a fundamental commitment to religious programming. (It is worth noting that for decades the BBC World Service was the only major external, international broadcaster to have a dedicated religious programmes department or run regular religious programmes — Voice of America has only recently begun to introduce some religious broadcasting. Domestically, the BBC is unique among major broadcasters in having a specialist religious broadcasting department. This is to be valued.)

Who is the audience for religious broadcasting? It is obviously much broader than those represented by faith-communities and religious groups. It could be defined as 'the 70% who believe in God in our society'. Or we could expand that definition to include the majority of the rest, who just 'don't know'.

In fact, the audience is just about everybody. Religious broadcasting is of course available to all, but it is important to recognise that religion itself is not just the province of those who are religious. Recognition of that fact is an important component of the philosophy of public service religious broadcasting. That might come as a shock to some Christians. Bob McLeish reminded us in the first chapter that the purpose of broadcasting is not just to serve either the politically powerful or the commercially powerful. And I shall add what he implied: that neither is it to serve the religiously powerful.

Virtues

What might we describe as public service religious broadcasting's virtues? I think there are many, and include:

First of all, *it is non-sectarian and non-partisan*. It has a judicious role in providing a platform for many religions and the faith-communities present in our democratic society. Public service broadcasting is not the exclusive property of any one of them.

Second, *it is non-proselytising*, at least in the sense that tele-evangelists would like it to proselytise.

Third, *it does not allow fund-raising* by religious groups.

Fourth, *it has an ability, precisely because it is not bound to any particular faith, to speak uncomfortable words*. To quote Bob McLeish again, 'a friend has a right to tell me things I don't like'.

A fifth virtue is that *public service broadcast religion can carry out investigative journalism within different faith-communities and religious groups*, precisely because it is not aligned with any specific religious group. It can even produce some investigative documentaries that the communities could not have produced themselves. A documentary series entitled *What Do Jews Believe?*[2] would clearly be less than representative if it were made only by one of the strictest Jewish traditions. But journalists within public service broadcasting can go into all sections of the Jewish community and ask a wide range of questions about their beliefs and fairly represent the spectrum of opinion and commitment on the issues.

A sixth virtue is that *public service broadcasting can create a space in which people who will not actually speak to each other, who represent different faiths and opinions (even within the same community) can hear each other*. They can have the opportunity, without the pressure of confrontation with the person who radically disagrees with them, of hearing what the other side thinks (provided, of course, that they don't switch off the radio or television). So it can offer debate and discussion and, within features and documentaries, can include people of different faiths and of different attitudes within faiths, who may never meet each other.

Achieving this can be a problem for 'confessional' broadcasters. The BBC and the ITV companies have an entrée. They can say, 'Can we interview you to be put in this documentary?' And people will more readily agree, because it's the BBC, ITV or Channel 4 who is asking. But if you are from a confessional broadcasting outlet, it may not be easy to invite people of other faith-communities to participate.

A seventh virtue is that *public service religious broadcasting can provide for the faith communities an insight into how other people see them*. This can be very valuable, if members of faith-communities are open and not defensive. It's right to complain when people in the

---

[2] *What Do Jews Believe?* was a documentary series produced by the author for BBC World Service, as part of a larger occasional series that focuses on the beliefs of Christians, Jews, Muslims, Hindus and Buddhists.

media get things wrong. But each of us ought to be prepared too, to stand back and say, 'Hang on a minute — these people may have a point! Isn't it interesting how they see us? Let's try to take that perception or criticism, and see how it can help to modify our behaviour.'

An eighth virtue is that *public service broadcast religious broadcasting can open up to us different worlds about which we knew nothing*. It may also be able to open up to us the religious beliefs and activities of our neighbours. Some Christians have been inside a mosque; the majority probably haven't. So it can be very instructive when we gain, through the medium of broadcasting, some understanding of how our neighbours in our culture behave in terms of their faith-commitments.

A ninth virtue is that *religious broadcasts can be a focus for the nation at times of crisis or significant moment*. For example, during the Gulf War the BBC broadcast a superb series of *Songs of Praise*. They scrapped the scheduled transmissions, and got Dr Colin Morris into Westminster Abbey. It was magisterial broadcasting, an example of the BBC's Religious Broadcasting Department reacting incredibly quickly, in order to echo something of our concerns of the moment within a religious context.

And a tenth virtue is that *public service religious broadcasting can also inform the uninformed*, often among broadcasters themselves.

Limitations

Yet, as we have already observed, public service religious broadcasting does have its limitations. There are a few deficiencies:

Religious programmes has to compete within the schedules to find an appropriate slot. This is a limitation — but it is also a blessing, because it is a defence against the more iniquitous consequences of the ratings war. If a broadcaster is required to carry a wide spectrum of programming, which in the public service broadcasting model includes religion, then such programmes are going to find a place. There can then be a public debate about where particular programme strands are scheduled, and there have been quite vociferous ones about some of the changes that the BBC and ITV have tried to make.

Sometimes *there do seem to be attitudes among those in authority within the BBC domestic services, that religion is either marginal or should be done away with*. As a result, a kind of defensiveness has been generated about religious programming within the BBC. (In the World Service the opposite is the case; the place of religious broadcasting is not questioned, because it is readily acknowledged that if you look at the world you cannot properly understand it without taking into account the religious dimensions.)

There is a danger that all religions will be seen as the same, and that their distinctives will not be identified. This is a danger; a more fundamental one is that public service religious broadcasting may allow different types of religion to be the subject or object of its output, but does not allow, from an editorial standpoint, the authentic committed voices and perspectives of the varied religious cultures in our society to have their own voices.

What I mean is this. Even if a producer has the most liberal interpretation of public service broadcasting, he or she is still the mediator, the gatekeeper. The public service broadcaster is still the editor, interposed between a particular religious group or point of view and what is broadcast to the audience.

We have to acknowledge, it's a limitation. I happen to think it's a fairly good one, but it does produce another problem: *public service religious broadcasting has a problem with advocacy.* I can go into a book shop and pick up religious books (or any other kind of book) and I can hear quite clearly (because somebody is speaking directly to me through the printed page) what their authors believe. But public service broadcasting, with the constraints under which it operates (and all of which I have described as positive public 'goods'), does have limitations in this area.

'CHRISTIAN' AND 'CONFESSIONAL' BROADCASTING

We now turn to 'confessional' broadcasting. By that I mean broadcasting undertaken by an agency or institution which has a faith commitment. In other words, a Christian-owned, or Jewish-owned, or Hindu-owned, or Muslim-owned broadcasting station. In the present context, because these are the London Lectures in Contemporary Christianity, I will look specifically at 'Christian broadcasting', though principles I outline can be equally applied to other faith-communities.

Let me introduce this section with a question. Why has 'Christian broadcasting' suddenly become so common a phenomenon? Premier

Radio (London Christian Broadcasting) has just started, and ARK 2, the television cable channel, is due in late 1996. There are several reasons.

The first is that there has always been within the church a genuine evangelistic desire to communicate the faith, and a desire to use all media available to achieve it.

The second is that new technologies mean more broadcasting outlets and opportunities. From the earliest days of broadcasting, one of the reasons for regulation was to control who had access to the technology and who had access to the airwaves. From the beginning, those have been controlled and regulated by government — for very good reasons. One important reason is the scarcity of frequency space. The International Telecommunications Union, through their world conferences, debate and allocate frequencies around the world. But that is changing — broadcasting is no longer limited to the use of terrestrial transmission frequencies. We now have cable, satellite, and other forms of communication which mean that there are a greater number of broadcasting outlets.

Thirdly, some of the faith-communities, including some very vocal Christian groups, have been dissatisfied with public service broadcasting and do not regard it very highly. There are those in the Christian community who look with envy and delight at the media opportunities available to Christians in the United States, and wish it could happen here.

Dangers

But there are dangers involved in such confessional broadcasting. One of them concerns funding. I have already argued that one of the constraints and one of the important virtues of public service broadcasting is that it is relatively independence from commercial pressures. A totally open market would bring with it the danger that those with the largest purse strings may come to dominate the religious broadcasting culture. Part of this discussion, of course, is the whole question of sponsorship. 'Who pays the piper calls the tune ...' — there are different kinds of sponsorship, but Christian broadcasting will have to face the issue of what their sponsorship actually means.

Accountability

The key to this debate is accountability. Public service broadcasting is accountable; to the public, to parliament and to others besides. With Christian broadcasting comes the question, to whom is it accountable? If a Christian broadcasting station is sponsored by some of the major churches, will it accept the risks of investigative journalism that reveals things, or produces challenges, which those sponsoring churches (or the broadcasters' other backers) may find embarrassing or uncomfortable?

This issue must be grappled with, particularly with documentaries and journalistic programmes — if, indeed, they decide to carry any. What do we do with those programmes that rightly investigate, explore, or draw attention to the sometimes unsavoury aspects of faith? There are many stories circulating at present: Roman Catholic priests' sexual activities, churches' and Christian agencies' investments in arms manufacturing, and many more. Will Christian broadcasters be free to investigate such stories and deal with such issues — or is part of their remit to be only 'positive'?

One of the things that impresses me about the Bible is the journalistic integrity of Scripture. It's a warts-and-all document. The New Testament is full of painful examples of corruption among the believers, including the apostles. Christian media outlets that attempt to present a sanitised Christian society will be failing in their duty to live up to the standards of Scripture. By the standards of journalistic honesty demonstrated in Scripture, particularly in the Gospels and Acts, much contemporary Christian media activity is found woefully wanting. The challenge for new Christian stations is not to repeat the faults of existing confessional media outlets which fail to take that kind of journalistic integrity on board.

And what about the activities of other faith-communities? In dealing with issues that relate to faith-communities that are not their own (if it decides to deal with such issues at all), Christian broadcasting will have to find a way through two potential pitfalls. The first is that of being seen as one faith-community merely attacking another; the second is that over-compensating and hence being unduly compromised. Public service religious broadcasting has the possibility of doing these stories properly precisely because it is not tied to any one faith-community or political group. That is the genius of its relative independence.

If Christian broadcasting is going to succeed in this country it will need to develop a 'Christian public service broadcasting' model. The irony is that it will need to emulate the best practices of public service broadcasting if it is to succeed, while at the same time eschewing tele-evangelism.

THE IMPORTANCE OF PUBLIC SERVICE RELIGIOUS BROADCASTING

From all this, I want to stress the importance of public service religious broadcasting. Public service broadcasting is a national asset; it is far too important to be dismissed or disregarded lightly. The revolution now taking place in broadcasting is not just a revolution of technology, but primarily a revolution in deregulation. I'm somewhat pessimistic about the future because I fear that the intellectual, political and social arguments that advocate judicious regulation, whether it be in the Cable Authority or wherever, are being lost through indifference. Those who ought to take their responsibilities seriously do not.

Some people assume that the onslaught of new technologies renders regulation redundant. That is not necessarily true. Let me just give one example. The Evangelical Alliance, in its 'Gagging the Churches' campaign of 1990 did the Christian community no service whatsoever. It elided all discussion about the nature and purpose of broadcasting culture and ecology in our society. The Alliance was more interested, or rather self-interested, in carving out of the broadcasting edifice something for itself. I believe that when we come to Christian broadcasting, the challenge for Christian citizens is to have a commitment, and a real commitment, to the broadcasting rights of other faiths too.

There are some people within the public service broadcasting culture who are completely antagonistic to any form of confessional broadcasting. I am not. I do, however, think that regulation is not only desirable but essential where it is possible. The commitment to bring in regulation that has some protections for our society as a whole does not limit freedom but promotes it. (There is an interesting parallel in the provision of confessional state schools in Britain, where we have Church Schools, Jewish schools and so on.)

It is possible to allow confessional broadcasters to work in a responsible, regulated way within our society. In fact other public service broadcasting models exist which do allow confessional mainstream programming. For example, the Netherlands has a public service broadcasting model with at least three confessional stations: NCRV (mainstream Protestant), KRO (Catholic) and EO (Evangelical). The basic motivation is to broadcast from a value system, rather than be committed to evangelism. The system is in the process of reform, but it is interesting that a society can fulfil a public service broadcasting remit and still have confessional stations.

Bob McLeish argued that public service broadcasting should cater for the whole person and relate to all society's needs and aspirations, therefore it is important that the spiritual and the realm of religion must always be part of public service broadcasting. Some Christians speak as if confessional broadcasting is the only way Christians should participate in broadcasting. They are throwing all their eggs into one basket. It is fundamentally irresponsible for Christians to do so without regard for the riches of our public service broadcasting culture. One of the important things about public service broadcasting is servanthood. That means that Christians have to work in the service of others, and those 'others' include all people who do not share our faith.

I'm committed to a secular model of the state, and therefore a secular broadcasting culture. By that, I mean broadcasting that is not in the control of any one religious group or party. This does not imply, as some in the United States would have it, that public institutions should be emptied of all religious perspective and content. It does imply that secular institutions like broadcasting should allow for the flowering of all and any faith-communities who act within the law, without favour.

Those who have written the obituary of public service broadcasting are very premature. In the United States they have had an 'open and free broadcasting culture' with a multiplicity of broadcasting stations and channels, but the great majority of viewers still watch the three major networks. And in this country public service broadcasting is going to take a vast majority of the audience for decades to come, whatever else is broadcast on cable and satellite. In this more open broadcasting culture, of course, you cannot stop people making choices. Some of us might find some choices on offer unpalatable. Those of us with major reservations about tele-evangelism broadcasting might be concerned that if such programmes were made more freely available, more people would choose to watch them. But the real battle for Christian citizens is to make sure that viewers and listeners have the opportunity of making *real choices*, by ensuring that there is adequate religious broadcasting as an alternative to tele-evangelists and 'confessional' broadcasters. That will be one of the strengths of public service broadcasting in the future when it comes to religious broadcasting. One, that it exists; and secondly, that it provides a real choice for the listener and viewer.

Dangers

There is however the danger that a proliferation of confessional broadcasters will lead the current bearers of the public service broadcasting torch (BBC, ITV, IRN, Channel 4, S4C and so on) to drop religious programming. That is exactly what has happened in the United States: religious programmes are virtually non-existent on the three major networks. This too should be a major concern for all Christians. Jim Mc'Donnell, the Director of the Catholic Centre for Communication, said that, 'If religious broadcasting is pushed to the margins [of public service broadcasting radio and television schedules] it will find it almost impossible to reach the majority of the non-church-going public.'[3]

There are a great many people who watch and listen to religious broadcasting. In any one month 60% of the British population are reached by religious broadcasting. That is staggering; public service broadcast religion is not a marginal matter. But there are other dangers facing public service broadcast religion which should be noted, such as public service broadcasters who appoint editors to religious strand programming who have no expertise whatsoever in religious affairs. There is a danger of misguidedly trying to make religious programmes more acceptable or popular by disguising religious content until an audience would be hard pushed to find any religion in them at all.

Religious programmes empty of all spiritual or religious content are the consequence of religious producers failing to take up the creative challenge of making their programmes interesting, watchable, listenable-to. A recent *Sunday Telegraph* television listing observed that 'while any lingering religious brief stays inoffensively

---

[3] Jim McDonnell, 'I Believe in Public Service Broadcasting' in: Peter Elvy (ed.), op. cit., p. 123.

in the background, [*Everyman*] at least remains a series of taking serious secular issues seriously'. Of course *Everyman* does make superb documentaries and has a team of excellent programme-makers. But some have been so devoid of religious content they might have been more appropriately placed in other programme slots.

Then there's the danger of turning the BBC Religious Broadcasting Department into the BBC Ethics Department. And there is also the danger that while we public service broadcasters at times justifiably criticise particular aspects of Christian and church practice, we can be benignly naive and uncritical of other faiths.

There is the further danger that some people are so ignorant of other faiths that prejudice rules the day. Think for example of some of the quite outrageous things that have been said in the media as a whole about the Islamic faith. There is a real discussion waiting to be had about Islam's strengths, weaknesses, and some of the horrendous things that go on in the name of that faith and culture (just as they do in Christian cultures), which is the result of honest investigation — not prejudice.

MAKING RELIGIOUS BROADCASTING RELEVANT AND ACCOUNTABLE

Another danger for public service religious broadcasting is the occasional failure of those of us within broadcasting to convince programme controllers of the importance and value of religious broadcasting. So often we refrain from putting up an idea because we 'know' that the controllers won't like it. We should be bombarding them with ideas until they have to take us seriously because they're good ideas which are going to going to be implemented by very good and competent programme makers. By so doing, we would also be getting the message across that religion just isn't marginal and we'd be subverting the assumption that it is.

Public service broadcasting has the further deficiency that sometimes it's not very good at allowing people to speak for themselves. It can sometimes undervalue personal religious experience. Time and time again, people are not being heard just talking very naturally about what their faith means in certain situations. Compare this with *Sport on 4* on Saturday mornings. There you can hear a vast number of sportsmen and sportswomen talking about everything under the sun. Even if you aren't interested in sport at all, you are aware that sport is something that is talked about, that people have experiences to share. We have to admit that we are sometimes a little nervous about allowing people to speak for themselves or about listening to people's personal, religious experience — and I don't only mean Christian experience.

If there has been a widely-felt dissatisfaction with religious broadcasting (and it is a big 'if'; I am not entirely convinced by those Christians who claim that there is, as part of their campaign for 'Christian' confessional broadcasting) then one can ask: 'Did we in public service religious broadcasting — especially within the BBC's Religious Programmes Department — do enough in the past to carry the audience with us?'. We should ask this particularly with respect to communities with a large vested interest; in other words, the adherents of all the major faiths.

How often we fail to carry our audience with us, or to explain what we are doing! It has been said already in this lecture series, that broadcasters can sometimes be arrogant. We have often been dismissive when people have expressed concern about religious broadcasting, and have been too defensive about what we have done. At times we have failed to make ourselves accountable. Obviously that does not mean that every complainant is right and that the BBC or ITV is always wrong. I am quite prepared to give an account and a defence of myself, and to point out quite clearly when I think a complainant is wrong. But I believe I owe it to every complainant to give an explanation. As broadcasters we must always remember that we are human and that we sometimes get it wrong, and we would ask you, our audience, to remember that this is so. We are not perfect!

In the end both public service religious broadcasting and Christian broadcasting (or any faith-committed, confessional broadcasting) have to face this question. To whom are they accountable? The public, the audience, the shareholders, the sponsors — who? I believe broadcasting must always be a service to and for others. Confessional broadcasting (Premier, ARK2 and others) is not only accountable to its own listeners and viewers. It is also accountable to the general public interest.

In conclusion, we must remind ourselves of the limits of all religious broadcasting. Dr Chris Arthur observed that 'while the aim of many media presentations may be to impart information about religion, the aim of religion itself is not information but redemptive transformation'.[4] Too often (in the Christian context) the limitations of religious broadcasting are forgotten, and there is an expectation that it should take on the mission of religious faith — redemptive transformation. And so my final plea, having spent so long in this lecture series talking about broadcasting, is this: remember that broadcasting cannot do everything. It is important, but its importance should not be allowed to get out of proportion. There is more to life than radio and television.

---

[4] Quoted by Jim McDonnell in ibid., p. 154.

INDEX OF NAMES AND TITLES

Bold numbers indicate either (in the case of contributors) the location of their chapter, or (in the case of biblical references) page numbers, in bold for clarity

ABC 30
Action News 46
After the Gold Rush (Henley Centre) 72
Alagiah, George 45, 70
Anglia TV 30
Apple Corporation 29
ARK2 29f, 77, 85-86, 96, 102
Arthur, Chris **102f**
Arts Centre Group 20
Associated Newspapers 30
Associated Press 34
Austen, Jane, *Pride and Prejudice* (1813) 12

Bad News 91
Band Aid 41
Barings Bank 40
Bartle, Bogle and Hegarty 80
BBC:
    Adult Education Department 74
    Adult Literacy Basic Skills Unit 80
    BBC 1 Literacy Campaign (1995) 80
    BBC 2 88
    BBC Bulletin Board 82
    BBC Now (information service) 32
    Broadcasting Support Services 75f
    Continuing Education Dept 74
    Controller of Radio 3 (and later Controller of Future Policy), Stephen Hearst 66
Department of Education 74, 80,82
Digital Audio Broadcasting 32
Director Generals: John Birt 30; Charles Curran 53; Alasdair Milne **3**; Deputy Director General, Alan Protheroe **3**
'Extending Choice in the Digital Age' (1995) 28
Guidelines on reporting crime 49
Head of Drama, Head of Sport 74
Internal study on staff progress (1987) 15f
Internet: Networking Club 82
Management Training Service (later, Department) **3**
Managing Director of Radio, David Hatch 64
Programme Complaints Unit 45
Programmes *see* names of programmes e.g. *Money Programme*
Radio London, BBC 25
Radio 1 66, 74; Radio 2 63-64; Radio 3 24, 63; Radio 4 19, 35, 42, 63, 74; Radio 5 Live 27, 36, 43
Regions 17
Religious Advisory Committee 91
Religious Broadcasting Department 94, 101, 102
Schools Department 74
Senior Management Conference 2f
Television Schools Department 74

Ukrainian Language Service 59
'Uplands Courses' (Management training seminars) 65ff
World Service 9, 23, 54-73 passim, 95; 1991 Annual Report 61
World University Network, proposed 81
Beamish Stout 88
Beckett, Margaret 41
Bellah, Robert N. *et al., The Good Society* (1992) 72
Berlin Wall 49
Bible, biblical references see names of Bible books
Birt, John 30
Black Wednesday 40
Blockbuster Entertainment 30
Bomber (BBC Radio 4) 19
Britain in the World Conference 60
British Council 81
British Sky Broadcasting (BSB) *see* Sky Broadcasting
British Telecom 27
Broadcasting Act (1996) 31-33
Broadcasting Research 56
Broadcasting Standards Council and Complaints Commission 45
Brookside 77
Buddhists 42
Buerk, Michael 41
Burmese listeners, two 60

Cable Authority 98
Canada-Spain fish dispute (1995) 51
Cantona, Eric 37, 47
Capital Radio 25; Capital Gold 25
'Carry On' films 43
CBN *see* Christian Broadcasting Network
Channel One Television 30
Channel 4, S4C, 76, 78, 82, 86, 88, 93
Channel 5 30
Christ, Jesus *see* Jesus
Christ and the Media (Muggeridge) 53, 72
Christian Broadcasting Network (CBN) 90

Christian Research Association, 1990 poll 9
Chronicles, I, 21:1-3 71
Church of England Newspaper 53
Churchill, Winston 91
Clark, David W. 89f
Classic FM 26
CNN 9, 27, 34, 35
Comic Relief 41
Commonwealth Broadcasting Secretariat (later, Association) 2
Compaq 29
Coronation Street 33, 66
Correspondent 46
Country music station 26
Curran, Charles 53
Cyberia 34

Daily Herald 70
Daily Mirror 11, 70 *see also* Mirror Group
Daily Telegraph 34
Dallas 48
David 71
Dean, Tim **87-103**
Devenport, Mark 36, 43
Diana, Princess of Wales 37
Dickens, Charles, *A Tale of Two Cities* (1859) 51
Diet Coke 88
Digital Audio Broadcasting 32
Disney Corporation 30
Do the Right Thing 83

Eastenders 33, 77
Edwards, Buster 49
English Church Census 77
EO (Dutch broadcaster) 99
Eurosport 89
Evangelical Alliance, 'Gagging the Churches' campaign (1990) 98
Evening Standard 73
Everyman 101
Ewing, J. R. 48

Financial Times 30
Financial World Tonight 35

First Tuesday 46
Forrest, John 42
From Our Own Correspondent 46
FTSE Index 42
Future Shock (Toffler) 15

Gale, George 42
Genesis 1 21
Gillard, Frank 2
Good Society, The (Bellah *et al.*) 72
Gospel *see* Gospel writer, e.g. John, Gospel of
Grade, Michael 8
Grundy International 30
G7 Summit (1987) 35
Guardian, The 34
Gulf War 94

Hatch, David 64
Hawtrey, Charles 43
Hayes, Brian 42
Hearst, Stephen 66
Heart (radio) 26
Henley Centre, *After the Gold Rush* (1994) 72
Here and Now 46
Hindus 95
Hiroshima 35
Hoddinott, John 73
Hofmeyr, Bremer 63-64
Holy Spirit 14
Hutton, Will, *The State We're In* (1995) 72

IBAR (BBC research department) 57
ILR *see* Independent Local Radio
Independent Broadcasting Authority 89
Independent Local Radio (ILR) 15, 88
Independent Television Commission 45
International Telecommunications Union 96
Inspector Morse 88
Internet 14, 29, 30, 34ff, 75
IRA 36, 43

Isaacs, Jeremy 70
Ishiguro, Kazuo, *Remains of the Day* (1989) 4
ITN 27
ITV Movies 88

James, Sid 43
James Cameron Memorial Lecture (1994) 55; (1996) 69-70
Jazz FM 25
Jeeves 5
Jerusalem Trust 20
Jesus 1-22 passim, 6-7, 12, 38ff, 48, 51-52, 70f, 73; and passim
Jews 91, 95, 98
JFM (radio) 26
John, Gospel of 1:14 22: compared to *Match of the Day* 12

Katz, John 34
Keane, Fergal 36, 45
Kendall, Bridget 35
Kershaw, Andy 63
Kiss (radio) 25, 26
Kray, Ronnie 49
KRO (Dutch broadcaster) 99

Langley, Stewart 72
Laurillard, Di 81f
Liddy, G. Gordon 44
Life in the Freezer 79
Limbaugh, Rush 44
Live TV 29f
London Broadcasting Company (LBC radio) 25, 42; LBC Newstalk, London Talkback 25
London Greek Radio 26
Los Angeles earthquake 34
Luke, Gospel of, 13:1-9 38
Lustig, Robert 35

McDonnell, Jim 100
McKenna, Virginia 63
McLeish, Robert **1-22**, 24, 83, 87, 91, 92f, 99; *Radio Production* (1994) 4
MAI 30
Major, John 41

Mandela, Nelson 36
'Marshall Plan for the mind' 66-67
Match of the Day 12
Matheson, George 63f
MBL (UK research agency) 61
MCI 30
Media Awareness Project 20
Melody (radio) 25, 26
Menneer, Peter 56
Meridian 30
Metro (radio) 15
Microsoft 27, 30
Milne, Alasdair 3
Mirror Group 29
Money Programme 27
More Bad News 91
Morris, Colin 22, 94
Moses 26, 84
MTV 29, 89
Muggeridge, Malcolm 1, 20, 53, 72; *Christ and the Media* (1977) 53, 72
Murdoch, Rupert 8, 27f
Music and Movement 78
Muslims 42, 85, 91, 95
Mutterbox 35f
Mytton, Graham **53-73**

Nash, Johnny 31
National Lottery 83
National Religious Broadcasters 90
Nazism 70
NBC 30
NCRV (Dutch broadcaster) 99
Neighbours 30, 66
Nepali listener, a 67
Newcastle 44
News at Ten 24, 46
News Bunny 29
News Corporation 30
News International 27, 28 *see also* Murdoch, Rupert
Newsnight 50
999 75
Nine O'Clock News 24
Noah 84
NOP survey on belief 77

Oklahoma bombing 9-10
Open Business School 79
Open University 77, 79, 81
Opportunities and Limitations 90

Paramount 30
Parliamentary Early Day Motion re BBC 60
Paul, St 59, 70f
Pearson Group 27, 30
Philippians 4:8-9 40
Philips (electronics) 29
Phillips, Justin **23-52**
Playboy 34
Polygram 29
Premier Radio 21, 26, 95, 96, 102
Press Association 2
Pride and Prejudice (Austen) 12
Princess Diana *see* Diana, Princess of Wales
Prisoner Cell Block H 30
Protheroe, Alan 3
Proverbs 14
Puttnam, David 81

Question of Sport, A 75

Radio 1, 2, 3, 4, 5 Live *see* BBC: Radio 1 . . .
Radio Authority 26
Radio Festival, Birmingham 1996 32
Radio Production (McLeish) 4
Radio programmes *see* name of programme, e.g. *Today*
Radio Times 63
RAI (Italy) 57
Really Bad News 91
Reap the Whirlwind 35
Redhead, Brian 24
Rees, Roger 63-64
Regent University 89f
Reith, John 72, 75, 82, 89
Remains of the Day (Ishiguro) 4
Reuters 27
Robertson, Pat 90
Rogers, Alan **74-86**
Rugby League 31

Index of Names and Titles

Sainsbury 29
Samaritan, the good 84
Save a Life 75
Seeds of Faith 63-64
Siepmann, Charles 56
Silvey, Robert 57n, 60; *Who's Listening?* (1974) 60
Simpson , O. J. 44
Sky Broadcasting, BSkyB 28, 33; Sky News 27
Smith, John (Labour Leader) 41
Songs of Praise 94
Sony Awards 36, 43, 63
South Sea Bubble 40
Spain, conflict with Canada over fish (1995) 51
Spectrum Radio 25, 26
Sport on 4 102
State We Ære In, The (Hutton) 72
Steven, Stuart 73
Sun, The 28, 70
Sunday Telegraph, The 100
Sutherland, Thomas 60

Tale of Two Cities, A (Dickens) 51
Talk Radio UK 26, 42, 45
Television programmes *see* name of programme, e.g. *Match of the Day*
Tesco 29
Thames TV 30
This Week 46
Time Warner 27, 34
Times, The 28, 34
Timpson, John 24
Today (Radio 4) 24, 35

Toffler, Alvin, *Future Shock* (1970) 15
Tokyo, investment vs Africa 47-48
Tomorrow's World 79
Top Gear 75
Tower of Babel 25
Tusa, John, James Cameron Memorial Lecture (1994) 55, 70

V-E Day celebrations 69
Viacom 30
Virgin FM 26
Visions of Heaven and Hell 47
Viva! (radio) 26
Voice of America 9, 92

Waite, Terry 60
Wall Street Crash 40
Watch 79
We Believe 42
What Do Jews Believe? 93
Who's Listening? (Silvey) 60
Willow Creek 84
Windows 95 (Microsoft) 30
Wodehouse, P. G. 5
Wooldridge, Mike 41
Words and Pictures 79
World in Action 46
World Service, BBC *see* BBC: World Service
World Tonight, The 35, 50
World University Network, proposed 81

Yeomans, Keith 78